Harvard Business Review

ON

BRAND
MANAGEMENT

D0169676

THE HARVARD BUSINESS REVIEW PAPERBACK SERIES

The series is designed to bring today's managers and professionals the fundamental information they need to stay competitive in a fast-moving world. From the preeminent thinkers whose work has defined an entire field to the rising stars who will redefine the way we think about business, here are the leading minds and landmark ideas that have established the *Harvard Business Review* as required reading for ambitious businesspeople in organizations around the globe.

Other books in the series:

Harvard Business Review on Breakthrough Thinking

Harvard Business Review on the Business Value of IT

Harvard Business Review on Change

Harvard Business Review on Corporate Strategy

Harvard Business Review on Effective Communication

Harvard Business Review on Entrepreneurship

Harvard Business Review on Knowledge Management

Harvard Business Review on Leadership

Harvard Business Review on Managing High-Tech Industries

Harvard Business Review on Managing People

Harvard Business Review on Managing Uncertainty

Harvard Business Review on Measuring Corporate Performance

Harvard Business Review on Nonprofits

Harvard Business Review on Strategies for Growth

Harvard Business Review

ON

BRAND

MANAGEMENT

A HARVARD BUSINESS REVIEW PAPERBACK

The *Harvard Business Review* articles in this collection are available as individual reprints. Discounts apply to quantity purchases. For information and ordering, please contact Customer
Service, Harvard Business School Publishing, Boston, MA 02163.
Telephone: (617) 783-7500 or (800) 988-0886, 8 A.M. to 6 P.M.
Eastern Time, Monday through Friday. Fax: (617) 783-7555, 24
hours a day. E-mail: custserv@hbsp.harvard.edu.

Library of Congress Cataloging-in-Publication Data
Harvard business review on brand management.
        p.   cm.—(The Harvard business review paperback series)
    Contains articles previously published in the Harvard
business review.
    Includes index.
    ISBN 1-57851-144-5 (alk. paper)
    1. Brand name products.   I. Harvard business review.
II. Title: Brand management.   III. Series.
HD69.7H37   1999
658.8'27—dc21   99-18899
                                                            CIP

*The paper used in this publication meets the requirements of the
American National Standard for Permanence of Paper for Printed
Library Materials Z39.49-1984.*

Contents

Building Brands without Mass Media   1
ERICH JOACHIMSTHALER AND DAVID A. AAKER

Brands versus Private Labels: *Fighting to Win*   23
JOHN A. QUELCH AND DAVID HARDING

How Do You Grow a Premium Brand?   51
REGINA FAZIO MARUCA

Should You Take Your Brand to Where the
Action Is?   79
DAVID A. AAKER

Extend Profits, Not Product Lines   105
JOHN A. QUELCH AND DAVID KENNY

The Logic of Product-Line Extensions   127
PERSPECTIVES FROM THE EDITORS

Can This Brand Be Saved?   147
REGINA FAZIO MARUCA

Your Brand's Best Strategy   169
VIJAY VISHWANATH AND JONATHAN MARK

About the Contributors   189

Index   193

Harvard Business Review

ON

BRAND
MANAGEMENT

Building Brands without Mass Media

ERICH JOACHIMSTHALER AND

DAVID A. AAKER

Executive Summary

COSTS, MARKET FRAGMENTATION, and new media channels that let customers bypass advertisements seem to be in league against the old ways of marketing. Relying on mass media campaigns to build strong brands may be a thing of the past.

Several companies in Europe, making a virtue of necessity, have come up with alternative brand-building approaches and are blazing a trail in the post-mass-media age. In England, Nestlé's Buitoni brand grew through programs that taught the English how to cook Italian food. The Body Shop garnered loyalty with its support of environmental and social causes. Cadbury funded a theme park, tied to its history in the chocolate business. Häagen-Dazs opened posh ice-cream parlors and got itself featured by name on the menus of fine

1

restaurants. Hugo Boss and Swatch backed athletic or cultural events that became associated with their brands.

The various campaigns shared characteristics that could serve as guidelines for any company hoping to build a successful brand: senior managers were closely involved with brand-building efforts; the companies recognized the importance of clarifying their core brand identity; and they made sure that all their efforts to gain visibility were tied to that core identity.

Studying the methods of companies outside one's own industry and country can be instructive for managers. Pilot testing and the use of a single continuous measure of brand equity also help managers get the most out of novel approaches in their ever more competitive world.

IF YOU TAKE AS A GIVEN—and we do—that companies must build strong brands to be competitive, then you are faced with a simple yet staggering challenge: How?

In the United States, mass-media advertising has long been the cornerstone of most brand-building efforts. But that norm is threatening to become obsolete. Fragmentation and rising costs are already inhibiting marketing through traditional mass media like television. And new communication channels—which, in some cases, allow individuals to bypass advertising as they peruse entertainment options, obtain information, or shop—are already in use.

Perhaps the new media scene will take more time to develop than the two or three years that the pundits have predicted. Perhaps it will not affect everyone: some people may not want (or may not be able) to pay to access ad-free media. It is not hard to imagine, however, that the media landscape as a whole will be very different in only a few years.

To build strong brands in this uncertain environment, U.S.-based companies would do well to study their counterparts in Europe. Because they were forced to, companies in Europe have long operated in a context that seems to mirror some of the harsher realities of the post-mass-media era. Media options for branded manufacturers in Europe historically have been limited and relatively ineffective. Europeans have had access to fewer commercial television stations, many of which bundle advertisements to avoid program interruptions. It is still rare to see media spanning several countries, despite the hype. What's more, because of the limited media availability, costs have been high. Even as new cable and satellite television channels were gradually added in European countries, costs did not decline—in part because new brands added to the demand. And powerful retailers in many nations usurp much of the available media capacity to engage in corporate advertising and to strengthen their private-label efforts.

In short, managers of brands in Europe have found that communication through traditional mass media has been ineffective, inefficient, and costly. As a result, many European-based companies have long relied on alternative communication channels to create product awareness, convey brand associations, and develop loyal customer bases. Their brand-building approaches may point the way for others to succeed in the new media age.

Here we focus on the approaches of six companies: the Body Shop, Hugo Boss, Cadbury-Schweppes with its Cadbury chocolate line, Nestlé with its Buitoni brand,

Grand Met with its Häagen-Dazs brand, and SMH with Swatch. Drawing on and extrapolating from those approaches, we have developed guidelines that we believe will serve all companies well, regardless of their location, their ability to access traditional mass media, or their desire and ability to involve themselves in the as-yet-undefined new-media opportunities.

Let Brand Strategy Drive Your Business Strategy

The successful European companies we've studied share one critical characteristic in addition to their reliance on alternative media: senior managers drive the brand building. They actively make brand building part of their strategic plans and, as a result, integrate their alternative approaches to brand building into their overall concept of the brand.

One such manager is the Body Shop's founder and CEO, Anita Roddick, who, believing that advertising is wasteful, has made her alternative brand-building methods the basis of her company's strategy. Peter Brabeck, the newly appointed CEO of Nestlé, is another example. Five years ago, Brabeck, as executive vice president for global foods, was the champion for the Buitoni brand; his involvement helped launch one of the food industry's most original experiments to bypass retailers and communicate directly with consumers. Another case is Jochen Holy, who with his brother shared the responsibilities of CEO at Hugo Boss between 1972 and 1993 and who became its main brand-builder. A grandnephew of the founder, Holy shaped the identity of the Hugo Boss brand and the communication of that identity.

In contrast, many U.S. companies delegate the development of brand strategy to someone who lacks the clout and incentives to think strategically. Or they pass the task to an advertising agency. Relying on an agency leads to two problems. First, in most cases, it creates a distance between senior managers and their key asset, the brand—the driver of future growth opportunities. That distance can make the coordination of communication efforts difficult—a situation that can result in confusion for customers, loss of synergy, and, ultimately, performance that falls short of potential.

Second, most agencies' talents, incentives, and inclinations still lead them to rely on mass-media advertising as their primary brand-building device. Agencies rarely suggest that a client lead brand building with alternative media. Although some agencies recently have made strides in expanding their ability to develop alternative-media options, most are still oriented toward advertising campaigns, despite pronouncements to the contrary.

Certainly, agencies have much to contribute strategically and tactically. However, the key to engaging in a broad, coordinated brand-building effort that accesses alternative media is to develop and control brand strategy inside the organization.

Clarify Your Brand's Identity

The identity of the brand—the brand concept from the brand owner's perspective—is the foundation of any good brand-building program. Whether pursuing alternative brand-building approaches, accessing multiple media, or both, a company must have a clear brand identity with depth and texture so that those designing and implementing the communications programs do not inadvertently send conflicting or confusing messages to customers. Unfortunately, many U.S. companies do not have a single, shared vision of their brand's identity. Instead, the brand is allowed to drift, driven by the often changing tactical communication objectives of product or market managers.

A clear and effective brand identity, one for which there is understanding and buy-in throughout the organization, should be linked to the business's vision and its organizational culture and values. It should provide guidance as to which programs and communications will support and reinforce the brand and which will detract and confuse. Knowing when to say no is critical. A brand identity that is so ambiguous and general that almost any kind of customer communication can be deemed suitable is not helpful.

Each of the six companies we examine subscribes to the idea of a strong, clear brand identity. But the Body Shop and Häagen-Dazs illustrate the concept particularly well.

The Body Shop's core brand identity is in essence its *profits-with-a-principle* philosophy. The soul of the brand, the philosophy sends a clear message to employees and customers alike. Consider how the company—in spite of the criticisms of its detractors—"walks the walk" in terms of developing programs reflecting the core identity.[1] The company opposes testing on animals, helps third-world economies through its Trade, Not Aid mission, contributes to rain forest preservation efforts, is active in women's issues, and sets an example for recycling. It participates in Save the Whales rallies, advocates for other endangered species (a line of its children's bath products, for example, comes with informative storybooks about various endangered animals), and supports the development of alternative energy sources. One summer, employees and supporters sent 500,000 signatures to the president of Brazil to urge him to stop the burning of trees there.

These efforts are not ancillary to the Body Shop brand; they are the brand. And the vision carries right through the customers' in-store experience. Enter a Body Shop, and you are greeted by a clerk who not only wears a Body Shop T-shirt bearing a social message but also believes in the company's causes, values, and products. Displayed among the store's goods and tester samples are posters and colorful handouts (printed on recycled paper) that provide information about the products, about social causes the company supports, and about how customers can get involved in rallies, social-cause advocacy groups, and the like.

Compare the Body Shop's brand identity with those of its competitors. Most skin care and cosmetic lines are indistinguishable, focusing on similar product attributes and health-and-beauty promises. And their customers are not involved with even their favorite brands—except to make a transaction or to receive a broadcast-style advertising message. Clearly, the Body Shop has transformed the skin care and cosmetics experience into something more than it has ever been.

Now consider Häagen-Dazs. Grand Met launched Häagen-Dazs in Europe in 1989 despite an economic recession, a tired, stagnant category, and established competitors. Unilever, Nestlé, Mars, and a great number of small but strong local ice-cream manufacturers such as Schöller in Germany, Mövenpick in Switzerland, and Sagit in Italy—advertised extensively, had high levels of name recognition, and controlled the limited freezer space in European supermarkets. In countries such as the United Kingdom, strong private labels held more than 40% of the take-home market. What's more, Häagen-Dazs was launched at a price 30% to 40% higher than its closest competitors and many times higher than the lower-priced products. How did it succeed? In part by being clear on what the brand stands for. The Häagen-Dazs brand means premium ice cream: thicker, creamier, and pricier than any other ice cream on the market; a sensual, self-indulgent, pleasurable treat targeted at sophisticated, affluent adult consumers.

The conventional way to introduce a new product such as Häagen-Dazs is to lead with a major advertising effort. But Grand Met chose a different route. To introduce the brand in Europe, it first opened several posh ice-cream parlors in prominent, affluent locations with heavy foot traffic. The cafélike stores, deliberately designed to contrast with the more traditional, sterile ice-cream parlors common in the United States, made a statement about Häagen-Dazs. The company also obtained placement for the ice cream in quality hotels and restaurants but stipulated that the Häagen-Dazs name be featured prominently on menus.

Häagen-Dazs pursued additional approaches to fuel word-of-mouth communications: branded freezers in food retail stores; sponsorship of cultural events; and a relatively low-budget, steamy print-media campaign with the theme The Ultimate Experience in Personal Pleasure. Linking the brand to arts sponsorship was a particularly savvy move. At one event, the Opera Factory's production of *Don Giovanni* in London, the ice cream was even incorporated into the show. When the

Don called for sorbet, he received a container of Häagen-Dazs. The result? A windfall of free publicity, begun and spread among target consumers.

The company's coordinated brand-building efforts were overwhelmingly successful. Häagen-Dazs brand awareness in the United Kingdom, for example, reached more than 50% within a few months. European sales of the product went from $10 million in 1990 to $130 million in 1994. Today the brand commands one-third of the market for top-of-the-line ice cream even though it continues to charge a hefty premium over copycat brands.

Whenever a clear and strong brand identity is lacking, a brand is like a ship without a rudder.

But when a clear and strong brand identity is lacking, a brand is like a ship without a rudder. Consider Farggi. In 1993, a Spanish company called Lacrem launched Farggi as a premium ice cream in Spain—one year after the arrival of Häagen-Dazs. The Farggi name was chosen because it sounded Italian and hence would evoke images of quality ice cream among Europeans. It also drew on the reputation of the successful Farggi line of pastry outlets. The problem was that the name had too many associations and messages. It had already been used for a standard-quality ice cream sold to food service establishments.

The Farggi strategy, confusing at best, had too many elements: competing directly with Häagen-Dazs, exploiting ties to Spain, having an Italian-sounding brand, and cashing in on the popularity of American-style ice cream. (The brand was positioned as being based on an authentic American recipe featuring the best-quality ingredients from Spain.)

Confusing messages were sent by Farggi's method of distribution as well. It said "premium" by offering the ice cream in 500-milliliter cups for two people (originally pioneered by Häagen-Dazs in Europe) through Farggi-owned or franchised ice-cream parlors reminiscent of nearby Häagen-Dazs stores. At the same time, it said "cut-price" by distributing Farggi through hypermarket stores in low-rent neighborhoods and through concessions at regional soccer stadiums.

In short, the brand was everything and nothing. And we believe that, ultimately, its muddled identity confused consumers and put them off. Not surprisingly, today Farggi is trailing Häagen-Dazs in Spain by a significant margin in both sales and market share.

Identity-Building Brand Exposure Creates Visibility

The role of visibility in creating brand equity is often underestimated. Simple recognition can affect perceptions: people tend to like known brands even if they have never used them. Brand visibility can signal leadership, success, quality, substance, and even excitement and energy—all before the product comes into play. However, strong brands find ways to achieve visibility by building and supporting the brand identity. Each of the companies we studied understood the importance of creating visibility while enhancing identity.

Hugo Boss, a fine clothier, created its image of exclusivity and high quality in large part through effective use of sponsorship. In the early 1970s, Hugo Boss sponsored Porsche in Formula One races to capitalize on Porsche's strong exclusive image and international presence. Over the years, the company also has taken on sponsorship of international tennis, golf, and ski competitions. It has funded exhibitions and artists, and it sponsored "Miami Vice" and "L.A. Law," both of which featured Hugo Boss garments.

Interestingly, Hugo Boss did not come into its own in terms of defining and building its brand until the 1980s. Although the company, founded in 1923 in the provincial town of Metzingen, Germany, was always a producer of high-quality clothing, the brand lacked flair. In the early 1970s, when the sons of Hugo Boss's brother became co-CEOs, annual revenues were only about 4 million deutsche marks. It was then that brand building began in earnest. A clear division of responsibility allowed fast action once a strategy had been determined.

The visibility garnered through Hugo Boss's sponsorships paid off quickly. Sales revenues topped DM 100 million in 1980 and increased tenfold during the 1980s. Hugo Boss's garments are sold in 57 countries, and more than half its sales come from outside Germany, with 20% generated outside Europe. In a 1991 study of men's clothing brands for the German magazine *Gehobener Lebensstil*, Hugo Boss was the highest ranked for having an aura of exclusivity and for having customers who routinely considered the brand when purchasing clothes.

If Hugo Boss's visibility campaign can be called inspired, SMH's efforts to build the Swatch brand are nothing short of brilliant. SMH took Swatch from rooftops to concert halls to ski slopes in a targeted campaign to boost visibility and forge a clear brand image, redefining a product category and reinvigorating the entire Swiss watch industry.

In the years just prior to the 1983 Swatch launch, watches were either low-cost time-measurement instruments or a high-cost combination of heirloom and investment. There was little in between. So SMH set out to define the Swatch core identity as a low-cost watch of excellent Swiss quality (rebuilding the good name of Swiss watch manufacturing) with a stylish, fun, youthful, provocative, and joyful brand personality. The concept of a fashion watch was born.

From the beginning, SMH made sure that Swatch messages were driven by that strong brand identity. For its launch in Germany, the company hung giant 165-meter "watches" from city skyscrapers with signs that read, "Swiss, Swatch, DM 60." In Spain and Japan, SMH used similar publicity stunts. For Swatch, the medium was, in part, the message in that it helped to communicate the brand identity.

Sponsorship, too, was carefully planned to bolster the brand's image among concentrated groups of potential target customers. In Breckenridge, Colorado, for example, Swatch backed skiing's Freestyle World Cup. In New York City, the company organized the Swatch World Break-Dancing Championship. In London, it sponsored Andrew Logan's Alternative Miss World show—and in Paris, a street-painting contest. The company also backed the traveling Museum of Unnatural History, supported the work of avant-garde musicians through the Swatch Impact Tour, and sponsored the pop art exhibition *L'heure est à l'art* in Brussels. Swatch quickly became part of the worldwide pop-culture movement.

The company also began linking new watch collections to carefully selected events. Although some collections have involved real product innovations, most are fashion driven, in keeping with the brand's concept.

Hence the company has sometimes tied introductions to such milestones as Halley's Comet, *perestroika*, the opening of Eastern Europe, and the 1992 United Nations Earth Summit in Rio de Janeiro.

SMH's brand-building efforts (which also include a highly successful customer-membership club) have generated tremendous brand awareness. Some of the company's limited-edition watches have even become collector's items, drawing exorbitant prices at Christie's and Sotheby's art-auction houses. In April 1992, sales reached 100 million, making Swatch the best-selling watch in history.

Keep in mind that sheer visibility should not be the ultimate goal in a serious brand-building effort: any campaign to increase visibility must have as its beacon the brand's identity. Without exception, the visibility-enhancing efforts of the companies we studied have been and continue to be consistent and supportive of their brand identities.

In contrast, the visibility efforts of the Italian clothing group Benetton illustrate the danger of activities that send the wrong message and do not express the brand identity. Founded in the 1960s, Benetton began with a coherent identity that conveyed youth, cultural diversity, racial harmony, and world peace; and it stayed directed for a long time. Then came the 1984 United Colors of Benetton campaign, which made use of print media, a Formula One sponsorship, and intensive in-store communication, including the distribution of one million copies of the customer magazine *Colors* through more than 7,000 stores worldwide.

Initially, the campaign was a great success. Sales of Benetton products grew rapidly. Over the years, however, Benetton's art director, the highly creative and talented photographer and artist Olivieri Toscani, developed his own style of advertising independent of the Benetton brand identity. He produced images for Benetton's communications campaigns that included a dying AIDS patient, a nun kissing a handsome priest, and a baby's bottom stamped "HIV Positive." Although very successful at creating publicity and visibility, Toscani's work appeared inconsistent with Benetton's established brand identity, and instead of building the brand and increasing sales, it alienated the target market and Benetton retailers.

The result was flat sales and a damaged brand. In Germany, Benetton's second-largest market, independent market research by Gruner & Jahr in 1992 and 1995 showed that, partly because of the controversial print-media campaign, awareness of Benetton had significantly increased relative to other clothing brands, but measures of likability relative to competing brands had decreased. Also in 1995, several of the 600 German retailers that used to carry the Benetton line banded together in a boycott. The group attributed much of its 1994 sales drop to the campaign. Germany's highest court eventually ruled against the controversial ads.

Involve the Customer in Brand-Building Experiences

Providing extensive information, especially using media advertising, cannot duplicate the impact of customers' personal experience with a brand. Consider the sampling program of Häagen-Dazs, the participation at Swatch events, the vicarious participation at Hugo Boss events, and the involvement of the Body Shop's customers in social activism. These experiences create a relationship that goes beyond the loyalty generated by any objective assessment of a brand's value. Cadbury's theme park in Bournville, England, and Nestlé's Casa Buitoni Club campaign are further illustrations.

Cadbury has taken what was once a simple chocolate-factory tour and turned it into a theme-park journey through the history of chocolate and the history of Cadbury—complete with a museum, a restaurant, a partial tour of the packaging plant, and a "chocolate event" store. Visitors, who are greeted and entertained by actors portraying Hernán Cortés, Montezuma, and King Charles II, learn about the origin of cocoa and chocolate, the life of the Mayan and Aztec Indians, how chocolate reached Europe, and how John Cadbury's empire began and grew.

Cadbury, a Quaker, began making chocolate nearly two centuries ago. Because of its Quaker heritage, his company pursued progressive ways of treating employees, and it became a model for social responsibility in the workplace. For many years, the Cadbury factory attracted visitors interested in seeing not only how chocolate was made but also how to establish progressive labor relations.

Cadbury World vividly links the taste experience to the brand's history.

In the late 1960s, however, the company ended its regular tours because of concerns about costs and hygiene. It wasn't until the mid-1980s that the Cadbury board of directors began to think about how a new kind of tour might strengthen the Cadbury brand.

The idea took off. The company invested £5.8 million to build Cadbury World, which opened its doors on August 14, 1990. For visitors, the Cadbury brand became something more than the product. True, the theme park offers hundreds of opportunities to sample the company's extensive line of chocolate products. But, more important, Cadbury World vividly links the taste experience to the brand's history.

Every year for the last three years, more than 450,000 people have visited the park, creating an operational profit. Cadbury has gained additional brand building through press coverage and word of mouth. Outside interests such as regional tourist boards, hotel chains, and the British Railways Board also have publicized the park to promote their own advantage. Undoubtedly, Cadbury World's success contributed to the 1996 naming of Cadbury as the most admired company in the United Kingdom. Although most companies would not consider building a theme park around their product, they can certainly learn something from Cadbury World—namely, that an entertaining, heritage-linked experience can be a cornerstone of brand building.

Nestlé-owned Buitoni, a 169-year-old Italian pasta company and brand, had a different but equally creative approach. Already available in the United Kingdom for 30 years, Buitoni was acquired by Nestlé of Vevey, Switzerland, in 1988. In the early 1990s, only 100 million pounds of pasta were sold in the United Kingdom—a per capita consumption one-fourth the size of that in the United States. Buitoni, with a leading share of 18%, faced two challenges. First, private labels, which held a total of 60% of the market, were a growing threat. Second, consumers did not seem to have a wide variety of pasta recipes in their repertoires. Buitoni perceived a need to expand consumers' use of the product, but in a way that benefited its own brand and not its competitors' brands.

Nestlé had successfully employed strategic business units to manage its worldwide corporate brands, including Buitoni, Maggi, Perrier, and seven others. Each business unit would create a global brand-identity plan. A country brand manager under a general country manager would develop and implement the brand plan for his or her territory, with the approval of the business unit. It was the United Kingdom's Buitoni brand manager—with support from the global brand manager—who in 1991 originally proposed a way to build a base of loyal Buitoni customers: the Casa Buitoni Club.

Nestlé's strategy was that Buitoni would become a helpful authority on Italian food—a brand and company to which consumers could turn for advice on the many varieties of pasta and their preparation. The company already had established a modern research facility in Sansepolcro, Tuscany—in the original Buitoni family villa—and a staff of chefs set out to experiment with new recipes and develop a wide array of new products.

The first stage of the Buitoni marketing effort, which took place in 1992 and 1993, was designed to strengthen brand awareness and create a core database of consumers interested in getting involved in Italian cooking. Buitoni gave free recipe booklets to anyone who responded to its offers, which were made in the press and through teletext or direct-response television. Other brand support in that initial stage included in-store sampling, sponsorship, a road show with many sampling activities, and public relations connected to the most popular running event in the United Kingdom, a half marathon. Total spending was £1.5 million in 1992 and £2.5 million in 1993. As much as 60% of the 1993 budget went into nonmedia forms of communications, as opposed to 40% in 1992. The integrated communications campaign (with the tag line Share the Italian Love of Food) resulted in a database of more than 200,000 consumers.

Then, in November 1993, the households in the database were invited to join the Casa Buitoni Club. Those responding received an Italian-lifestyle information packet and a full-color quarterly newsletter (with articles about Tuscany and other parts of Italy), pasta recipes, and discount vouchers. Membership benefits also included a toll-free number for anyone wanting cooking advice or suggestions. In addition, there were sweepstakes (with the prize of a visit to the original Casa Buitoni villa in Tuscany), gourmet-cooking weekends, the opportunity to sample new products, merchandise offered against proof of purchase, and suggestions on planning pasta feasts.

Since the club's inception, membership has grown steadily through word of mouth and marketing efforts in alternative low-cost channels, such as public relations events, promotions, and invitations on packages of Buitoni pasta. The use of Buitoni products and customers' loyalty have increased as well. The toll-free line builds relationships between the brand and club members and provides valuable customer feedback to the company. The Buitoni program in the United Kingdom has influenced the marketing of Buitoni in other countries (for example, Japan) and the strategies of other Nestlé brands (for example, Maggi).

There is brand-building power in getting the customer involved in a larger experience when using a product. Two other examples that illustrate that power are Adidas and Virgin. Adidas has developed what it calls *urban culture programs*, which include participatory events across Europe such as a streetball challenge, a streetball festival, and a track-and-field clinic. These popular events include not only athletics but also fashion shows, music (including a hip-hop band), and other entertainment. Spending significantly on this sort of brand building, Adidas has also obtained collaborators: major sports leagues; other marketers targeting the same youth segments as Adidas; sport celebrities; and, most important, media services, which cover events and hence provide free publicity. Partly because of its urban culture programs, Adidas has reversed (without media advertising) the decline in sales that started in the early 1980s. It has turned in two-digit growth figures and market share gains in the last several years—in the face of major media expenditures by Nike and Reebok. Indicators of brand perception show considerable improvements, especially among younger consumers.

Virgin's approach involved participating in CompuServe's U.K. Shopping Centre, a virtual mall. Subscribers who visit Virgin's Go Megastore can learn about and purchase CDs, videos, and computer games while having an involving and entertaining experience. The feel and experience of visiting the virtual store, coupled with the fact that Virgin was one of the first British retailers to use this medium, helps to reinforce the Virgin brand's associations of being innovative, pioneering, energetic, entertaining, and obsessed with providing value to customers.

Making It Happen

Interestingly, several of the companies we have discussed did not deliberately seek to pursue alternative brand-building methods instead of mass-media advertising. Instead, they were blessed, one might say, with liabilities that encouraged them to be creative. For example, even if Anita Roddick had been a proponent of traditional media advertising, the Body Shop simply lacked funds. Hugo Boss, lacking exclusivity, an international presence, and design credibility, knew that a mass-media campaign wouldn't change that. Nor would it convince the fashion world that a small company, with distribution in only a narrow segment of the German market, was a reason to think that "Germany" suddenly spelled style. Häagen-Dazs lacked access to the freezers of powerful retailers because Grand Met's food interests in Europe were relatively small. Traditional brand building would not have gotten freezers with the Häagen-Dazs logo into prime retail chains. And Swatch, at its launch, did not have the cost structure to mount a significant campaign against its Japanese competitors.

Although not everyone is blessed with such liabilities, the lessons these companies learned are valuable and transferable. Developing a set of alternative approaches to brand building isn't easy, however, particularly for companies that have long relied on media buys as the cornerstone of their brand-building efforts. But with dedication and commitment from senior managers, alternatives can be worth the time and investment.

We recommend that managers study the brand-building methods of companies outside their industry and outside their country. Creative approaches used by companies in other fields or other markets may suggest effective brand-building techniques that also provide differentiation from competitors.

In-house capability in the lead media is important for real and sustainable competitive advantage. If the lead-media implementation is outsourced, it easily can be copied. When it is actively managed internally, as was the case with the Buitoni direct-marketing effort, the Cadbury theme park, the Hugo Boss event-sponsorship program, the Swatch events, the Body Shop's activism, and the Häagen-Dazs sampling effort, then the resulting effectiveness and efficiency of the program can represent significant barriers to competitors.

One person or team inside the organization should have the responsibility for the brand. The charge is to create a strong, clear, rich identity and to make sure that the implementation groups, whether inside or outside the company, understand that identity. When alternatives to mass-media advertising are driving the brand-building process or playing a substantial role, it is particularly important to have a brand champion with the ability, authority, and incentive to ensure that the brand identity is being delivered consistently across multiple media.

We suggest pilot tests to learn firsthand what works and what does not and to gain confidence in programs that are novel and seem risky. The Swatch and Häagen-Dazs programs both benefited from pilot testing.

Finally, managers should monitor the results of the effort. A single and continuous measure of brand equity helps companies understand clearly the contribution of alternative-communication vehicles in building brands. And careful monitoring can reveal how to expand those vehicles to serve the company best.

Note

1. Any brand is vulnerable that has a strong and visible brand identity claiming unusually high standards. Thus,

when the Intel Pentium chip makes an arithmetic error under certain circumstances or a Body Shop program is seen to fall short of its profits-with-a-principle philosophy, those events create news.

Originally published in January–February 1997
Reprint 97107

Brands versus Private Labels

Fighting to Win

JOHN A. QUELCH AND DAVID HARDING

Executive Summary

HOW REAL IS the private-label threat to branded products? What should national-brand manufacturers do about it?

On the one hand, manufacturers have reason to be concerned. There are more private labels on the market than ever before; collectively, unit shares of store-brand goods place first, second, or third in 177 of 250 supermarket product categories in the United States. But many manufacturers have not fully recognized two important points in considering this threat.

First, private-label market share generally goes up when the economy is suffering and down in stronger economic periods. In the depth of the 1981–1982 recession, it peaked at 17% of sales; in 1994, when private labels received great media attention, it was more than two percentage points lower at 14.8%. Second, manufacturers of brand-name products can have significant influence on the seriousness of the challenge posed by private-label goods. In fact, in large part, they can control it.

It is difficult for managers to look at a competitive threat objectively and in a long-term context when day-to-day performance is suffering. But the authors strongly advocate keeping the private-label challenge in perspective. To help managers gain this perspective, they analyze recent developments that have boosted the private-label market. Then they highlight the considerable strengths of the brand name. Managers at brand manufacturers are cautioned about their own reliance on private-label production; those that have not entered that market are counseled not to do so. Finally, the authors offer winning strategies that manufacturers can use to fight private labels and maintain the long-term health of their brands.

You know the old joke: Just because you're paranoid doesn't mean they're not out to get you. In a nutshell, that describes how manufacturers of brand-name products react to competition from private labels. On one hand, manufacturers are right to be concerned: There are more private labels—"store-brand" goods—on the market than ever before. Collectively, private labels in the United States command higher unit shares than the strongest national brand in 77 of 250 supermarket product categories. And they are collectively second or third in 100 of those categories. But on the other hand, many manufacturers have overreacted to the threat posed by private labels without fully recognizing two salient points.

First, private-label strength generally varies with economic conditions. That is, private-label market share generally goes up when the economy is suffering and down in stronger economic periods. Over the past 20 years, private-label market share has averaged 14% of U.S. dollar supermarket sales. In the depth of the 1981–1982 recession, it peaked at 17% of sales; in 1994, when private labels received great media attention, it was more than two percentage points lower at 14.8%. Second, manufacturers of brand-name products can temper the challenge posed by private-label goods. In fact, in large part, they can control it: More than 50% of U.S. manufacturers of branded consumer packaged goods make private-label goods as well.

It is difficult for managers to look at a competitive threat objectively and in a long-term context when day-to-day performance is suffering. Examples of big-name brand manufacturers under pressure from private labels and generics aren't reassuring. What manager wouldn't worry when faced with the success story of Classic Cola, a private label made by Cott Corporation for J. Sainsbury supermarkets in the United Kingdom? Classic Cola was launched in April 1994 at a price 28% lower than Coca-Cola's. Today the private label accounts for 65% of total cola sales through Sainsbury's and for 15% of the U.K. cola market.

Reactions to private-label success can have major repercussions. Consider what happened in the week following Phillip Morris's announcement in April 1993 that it was going to cut the price of Marlboro cigarettes. Wall Street analysts interpreted the price cut as the death knell of brands; Philip Morris's stock lost $14 billion of its value; and the stocks of the top 25 consumer packaged-goods companies collectively lost $50 billion in value.

Although we agree that many national brands are under pressure—especially from the number three brand on down in each product category—we strongly believe that the private-label challenge must be kept in perspective. What's needed is an objective approach and the same careful consideration a company would give to any brand-name competitor. To begin, managers must consider whether the threat posed by private labels will grow or fade. Then, they must reconsider the strengths of the brand name: Brands are far from dead. Finally, if their companies already produce private-label goods, they should weigh the costs of competing in the generic market against the benefits. And if the companies have not entered that market, they probably shouldn't.

The Private-Label Threat

Several factors suggest that the private-label threat in the 1990s is serious and may stay that way regardless of economic conditions.

THE IMPROVED QUALITY OF PRIVATE-LABEL PRODUCTS

Ten years ago, there was a distinct gap in the level of quality between private-label and brand-name products. Today that gap has narrowed; private-label quality levels are much higher than ever before, and they are more consistent, especially in categories historically characterized by little product innovation. The distributors that contract for private-label production have improved their procurement processes and are more careful about monitoring quality.

THE DEVELOPMENT OF PREMIUM PRIVATE-LABEL BRANDS

Innovative retailers in North America have shown the rest of the trade how to develop a private-label line that delivers quality superior to that of national brands. Consider Loblaws' President's Choice line of 1,500 items, which includes the leading chocolate-chip cookie sold in Canada. As a result of careful, worldwide procurement, Loblaws can squeeze the national brands between its top-of-the-line President's Choice label and the regular Loblaws private-label line. And President's Choice has even expanded beyond Loblaws' store boundaries: Fifteen U.S. supermarket chains now sell President's Choice products as a premium private-label line.

Meeting the private-label challenge requires the same consideration a company would give to any other competitor.

EUROPEAN SUPERMARKETS' SUCCESS WITH PRIVATE LABELS

In European supermarkets, higher private-label sales result in higher average pretax profits. U.S. supermarkets average only 15% of sales from private labels; they average 2% pretax profits from all sales. By contrast, European grocery stores such as Sainsbury's, with 54% of its sales coming from private labels, and Tesco, with 41%, average 7% pretax profits.

Of course, the reasons for the strength of private labels in Europe are partly structural. First, regulated television markets mean that cumulative advertising for name brands has never approached U.S. levels. Second, national chains dominate grocery retailing in most west European countries, so retailers' power in relation to manufacturers' is greater than it is in the United States. In the United States, the largest single operator commands only 6% of national supermarket sales, and the top five account for a total of 21%. In the United Kingdom, by contrast, the top five chains account for 62% of national supermarket sales.

But growing numbers of U.S. retailers such as the Kroger Company believe that strong private-label programs can successfully differentiate their stores and cement shoppers' loyalty, thereby strengthening their positions with regard to brand-name manufacturers and increasing profitability. What's more, cash-rich European retailers like Ahold (a Dutch supermarket chain) and Sainsbury's have begun to acquire U.S. supermarket chains and may attempt to replicate their private-label programs in the United States.

THE EMERGENCE OF NEW CHANNELS

Mass merchandisers, warehouse clubs, and other channels account for a growing percentage of sales of dry groceries, household cleaning products, and health and beauty aids. Wal-Mart Stores, in fact, is already one of the top ten food retailers in the United States. Private labels accounted for 8.8% of sales at mass merchandisers in 1994; in some categories, that percentage was much higher. For example, 39% of soft-drink volume sold in mass merchandisers is private label versus 21% in supermarkets. Some national-brand manufacturers have encouraged the growth of new channels, but they may regret it later. Unlike supermarkets, mass merchandisers and warehouse clubs are national chains; they have the incentive to develop their own national brands through private-label lines, and they have the procurement clout to ensure consistent quality at low cost.

THE CREATION OF NEW CATEGORIES

Private labels are continually expanding into new and diverse categories. Their growth follows some general trends. (See "What Drives Private-Label Shares?" at the end of this article.) In supermarkets, for example, private labels have developed well beyond the traditional staples such as milk and canned peas to include health and beauty aids, paper products such as diapers, and soft drinks. Private-label sales have also increased in categories such as clothing and beer. With that expansion comes increased acceptance by consumers. The more quality private-label products on the market, the more readily will consumers choose a private label over a higher-priced name brand. Gone are the days when there was a stigma attached to buying private labels.

Brand Strength

Taken together, these trends may seem daunting to manufacturers of brand-name products. But they tell only half the story. The increased strength of private labels does not mean that we should write an obituary for national brands. Indeed, the brand is alive and reasonably healthy. It requires only dedicated management to thrive. Consider the following points.

The purchase process favors brand-name products.
Brand names exist because consumers still require an
assurance of quality when they do not have the time,
opportunity, or ability to inspect alternatives at the point
of sale. Brand names simplify the selection process in
cluttered product categories; in the time-pressured dual
income households of the 1990s, brands are needed more
than ever. In fact, a 1994 DDB Needham survey indicates
that 60% of consumers still agree that they prefer the
comfort, security, and value of a national brand over a
private label. Although this percentage is lower than the
75% figure common in the 1970s, it has remained fairly
constant during the last ten years.

**Brand-name goods have a solid foundation on
which to build current advantage.** Put simply,
brands have a running start. The strongest national
brands have built their consumer equities over decades
of advertising and through delivery of consistent quality.
From year to year, there is little change in consumers'
rankings of the strongest national brands. Forty of the
top 50 brands on Equitrend's consumer survey were the
same in 1993 as in 1991. In contrast, retailer brand
names are not prominent. On the 1995 Equitrend list of
the top 100 brands in the United States (based on rat-
ings of 2,000 brands), only 5 store brands appear, the
highest of which is Wal-Mart at number 52, down from
34 in 1994.

**Brand strength parallels the strength of the
economy.** As the United States has emerged from
recession, manufacturers of national brands have
increased advertising and won back some consumers
who had turned to private labels. Sales of premium-
quality, premium-priced brands are on the rise. A 1993

Roper Starch Worldwide survey found that 48% of packaged-goods buyers knew what brands they wanted before entering the store, up from 44% in 1991.

National brands have value for retailers. Retailers cannot afford to cast off national brands that consumers expect to find widely distributed; when a store does not carry a popular brand, consumers are put off and may switch stores. Retailers must not only stock but also promote, often at a loss, those popular national brands—such as Miracle Whip, Heinz ketchup and Campbell's soup—that consumers use to gauge overall store prices. Even if, in theory, retailers can make more profit per unit on private-label products, those products (with rare exceptions such as President's Choice chocolate-chip cookies) just do not have the traffic-building power of brand-name goods.

Excessive emphasis on private labels dilutes their strength. What could be more convenient, some retailers argue, than to have consumers remember a single store name? The problem is that stretching a store name—just like a manufacturer name—over too many product categories muddies the image. Many consumers rightly do not believe that a store can provide the same excellent quality for products across the board. Even Sears, Roebuck & Company, the premier private-label retailer in the United States, found it necessary to invest in category-specific sub-brands such as Craftsman and Kenmore—which, in turn, have been outgunned by more focused manufacturer brands such as Black & Decker and Sony. By the late 1980s, Sears' excessive emphasis on private labels led to consumers' perceptions that the retailer's assortment was incomplete as well as to reduced store traffic and poor profits. In 1990, the company launched the Sears Brand Central store-within-a-store concept and committed itself to stocking a full assortment of national brands alongside its private labels in electronics and appliances.

If You Don't, Don't Start

Faced with the pros and cons of private-label production, what should national-brand manufacturers do? Our recommendation to companies that do not yet make products for the private-label market is simple: Don't start.

Some brand-name manufacturers make private-label goods only to use occasional excess production capacity. In those circumstances, private-label production may seem tempting. But beware. Although the system may work well for a company for a time, private-label production can become a narcotic. A manufacturer that begins making private-label products to take up excess capacity may soon find itself taking orders for private-label goods in categories where the market share of its own brand is weak.

For manufacturers seeking only to use excess capacity, private-label production can eventually become a narcotic.

That step, too, may seem reasonable enough. Indeed, production managers may argue that in addition to using up excess capacity, private-label production can increase cumulative production experience and lower unit manufacturing and distribution costs. Heinz, for example, is a major supplier of private-label baby food. However, it is easy to slide down the slippery slope. The next step in the process is to supply private-label goods in categories that are the lifeblood of the manufacturer's branded sales. After all, the thinking goes, high-volume private-label orders placed well in advance of required delivery dates can help smooth production and take less time and effort per unit to sell than the company's own branded goods.

From that point, however, the results of those tactics are predictable: The company's strategy becomes confused; it starts to cannibalize its brand-name products; and it may even face financial disaster. Consider what happened to Borden. Once a strong manufacturer of well-known brands, Borden found itself floundering in the early 1990s largely because of a progressive, and eventually excessive, commitment to private-label manufacturing, which eroded its focus on sustaining its branded products. As a result of declining margins and cash flows, the company was finally sold to an investment firm in 1995.

Manufacturers still tempted by private-label production should understand, first, that managers invariably examine private-label production opportunities on an incremental marginal-cost basis. The fixed overhead costs associated with the excess capacity used to make the private-label products would be incurred anyway. But if private-label manufacturing were evaluated on a fully costed rather than on an incremental basis, it would, in many cases, appear much less profitable. (See the chart "The Real Costs of Private-Label Manufacturing.") The more private-label production grows as a percentage of total production, the more an analysis based on full costs becomes relevant.

Second, private-label production can result in additional manufacturing and distribution complexities that add costs rather than reduce them. For example, packages and labels have to be changed for each private-label customer, and inventory holding costs increase with each private-label contract.

Third, efficiencies of selling private-label contracts are also exaggerated. Whenever a private-label contract

---

The Real Costs of Private-Label Manufacturing

Every company producing private-label goods should answer three questions: What is the true contribution from private-label products? What fixed costs are attributable to private-label production? And how much will the private-label goods cannibalize the company's national brands?

At Consumer Corporation, the contribution from a popular food product was $0.40 per pound for the national brand and $0.23 per pound for the private label. Thus the company had to sell almost two pounds of the private-label product to equal the contribution generated by the sale of one pound of the national brand. If Consumer's national brand incurred "fair share" cannibalization—that is, a loss of share equal to that garnered by the private label—then the company would earn a marginal profit. In many cases, the cannibalization rate will be higher than fair share. In this example, Consumer decided that the risk outweighed the reward; it invested more in the branded product.

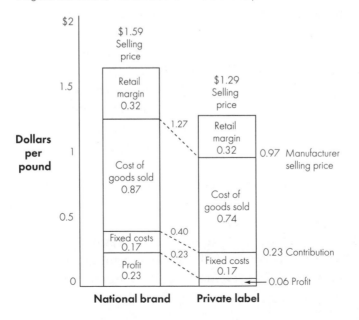

comes up for renewal, there is inevitably a long and arduous negotiation as competitors attempt to steal the business. And most retailers employ different buyers for national brands and private labels, so manufacturers must maintain two sales relationships with each retailer.

Fourth, it is easy to overstate the relative contribution of private-label goods and therefore to understate the cost of cannibalization. And even though selling private labels often requires a separate sales relationship, sales forces generally sell where they are most welcome; this means that invariably the private-label offerings end up in a manufacturer's strongest accounts, not the weakest.

Because private-label and national-brand manufacturing and marketing are based on such different cost structures, it's hard for one organization to do both well. Some companies try to manage both together to approach the trade with a total category solution, but this practice often leads to strategic schizophrenia, pressure from demanding retailers to give priority to less profitable private-label shipments, and unproductive use of management time in reducing conflicts.

Other organizations try to manage their private-label business in separate divisions to compete better with the lean cost structures of private-label-only manufacturers. In such organizations, private-label manufacturing cannot be contained, and inevitably the private-label goods cannibalize national-brand sales.

Proponents of private-label manufacturing suggest that it is necessary for competitive reasons. If one manufacturer refuses private-label contracts, another will take them, perhaps using the profits from private-label manufacture to support the marketing of its national brands. Since private-label purchasers represent a legitimate and continuing consumer segment in most product

categories, the goal of diversification argues for a manufacturer having a stake in both parts of the market. Proponents also argue that the dual manufacturer has more
ability to influence the category, the shelf-space allocation between national brands and private labels, the
price gap between them, and the timing of national-
brand promotions; and further, that its clout with the
trade is enhanced by supplying both national brands
and private labels. Moreover, they contend, the learning
about consumers and costs that comes from being in the
private-label market can enhance the manufacturer's
ability to defend its national brands. And again, considered alone or in a short-term context, these views can
seem compelling.

A few companies have used private-label production
effectively as a temporary strategy to enhance competitive advantage. In Europe, PepsiCo Foods International
succeeded in capturing private-label businesses from its
key competitor, forcing it to close plants and, more
importantly, weakening its national brands. In the
United States, General Electric Company used a two-
step process in the lightbulb business. It first captured
private-label trade contracts from competitors and then
proved through comparative in-store experiments that
trade accounts could make more money just stocking
GE lightbulbs than by stocking both GE and private-
label bulbs.

There is no evidence, however, that making private-
label products enhances a brand manufacturer's trade
relationships in the long run and results in preferential
merchandising support for its national brands. Far from
enhancing diversification, private-label contracts can
increase a brand manufacturer's dependence on a few
large trade accounts, force the manufacturer to disclose

its cost structure and share its latest product and process improvements, and result in margin pressure every time a contract is up for renewal. The president of a division of Consumer Corporation (not its real name)—a U.S. packaged-goods multinational competing in more than two dozen categories—was dismayed to find his plant shipping private-label product ahead of its own brands. When he asked why, he was told, "The stores are calling for their stock, not ours."

Evaluating Private-Label Business

If your company does produce private-label goods, it is important to assess their effect on the business as a whole and to keep private-label operations under control. Taking the following steps should help.

First, conduct a private-label audit. Amazingly, top-level executives at many companies do not know how much private-label business their organizations do. This ignorance is most evident in multinationals with far-flung operations that have grown rapidly through acquisitions—especially of businesses in Europe and Canada, where private-label penetration is strong. Often those companies' internal control systems do not accurately reflect private-label sales or the additional stockkeeping units devoted to them.

It is easy to overstate the contribution of private-label goods and to understate the cost of cannibalization.

Second, calculate private-label profitability on both a full-cost and marginal-cost basis. Analyses at Consumer found that on a full-cost basis its private-label business was unprofitable in almost all categories in the United

States. In Europe and Canada, however, where greater trade concentration results in higher retail prices for both national brands and private-label alternatives, the company found that its private-label business was mostly profitable. Armed with this information, Consumer implemented a new justification system for its private-label production. In effect, the burden of proof shifted from "why not" to "why." As a result, the company's private-label activity declined precipitously in the United States.

Third, examine the impact of private labels on the market shares of your national brands. Analysis of U.S. retail scanner data showed that private-label penetration had increased from 1991 to 1993 in 16 of Consumer's 24 categories, but in only 4 of them had private labels gained share by cannibalizing sales of Consumer's brands. In 14 categories, both Consumer and private-label producers had gained shares at the expense of weaker national brands; in most of these cases, Consumer's national brand was the market-share leader. This analysis suggested to Consumer that there was no need to make private-label goods to maintain market share in most of the categories in which it competed.

Finally, close excess capacity. The option of shutting down unused capacity is almost never considered in the private-label debate. Yet in five categories, Consumer found that the profitability of manufacturing rationalization (including exit costs) was superior to filling excess capacity with low-return private-label business.

Winning Strategies

We recommend that national-brand manufacturers take the following nine actions—whether they currently make private-label products or not—to stem any further share gains by private labels.

Invest in brand equities. This is not a new thought, but it is worthy of fresh consideration. For most consumer-goods companies, the brand names they own are their most important assets. James Burke, former CEO of Johnson & Johnson, has described a brand as "the capitalized value of the trust between a company and its customer." Brand equity—the added value that a brand name gives to the underlying product—must be carefully nurtured by each successive brand manager. Managers must continually monitor how consumers perceive the brand. Consistent, clear positioning— supported by periodic product improvements that keep the brand contemporary without distorting its funda- mental promise—is essential. For example, Procter & Gamble Company has made 70 separate improvements to Tide laundry detergent since its launch in 1956, but the brand's core promise that it will get clothes cleaner than any other product has never been compromised. Consistent investment in product improvements enhances a brand's perceived superiority, provides the basis for informative and provocative advertising, increases the brand's sustainable price premium over the competition, and raises the costs to private-label imitators who are constantly forced to play catch-up.

Innovate wisely. Desperate to increase sales and pres- ence on the shelves and to earn quick promotions, too many national-brand managers launch line extensions. Most are of marginal value to customers, dilute rather than enhance the core-brand franchise, add complexity and administrative costs, impair the accuracy of demand forecasts, and are unprofitable on a full-cost basis. In 1994, more than 20,000 new grocery products were introduced, half of them line extensions and 90% of them unlikely to survive through 1997. Too many line extensions confuse consumers, the trade, and the sales force, and reduce the manufacturer's credibility with the trade as an expert on the category. In addition, if line extensions fragment the business, the average retail sales per item will decline. That, in turn, opens the door for a private-label program that focuses just on a brand's best-sellers and therefore can deliver attractive average sales and profits per item.

Product-line extensions do make sense when a category has a large premium component and the level of rivalry is high. But in most instances, especially in commodity categories that are driven by price, product-line proliferation and innovation are a waste of money.

Use fighting brands sparingly. For similar reasons, managers should be wary of launching fighting brands, which are price positioned between private labels and the national brands they aim to defend. The purpose of a fighting brand is to avoid the huge contribution loss that would occur if a leading national brand tried to stem share losses to private labels by dropping its price; the fighting brand gives the price-sensitive consumer a low-cost branded alternative. Philip Morris has effectively used fighting brands L&M, Basic, and Chesterfield around the world to flank Marlboro. Likewise, Heinz has used fighting brands well in pet foods. However, the fighting brand can end up competing with the national brand for consumers who would not have switched to private-label products anyway. For this reason, Procter & Gamble recently phased out White Cloud toilet tissue and Oxydol laundry detergent. Rarely do fighting brands make money. At Consumer, fighting brands had close to $1 billion in revenues but were unprofitable after the allocation of fixed costs. The management time that these products absorb is often better invested in building the equity of the national brand.

Build trade relationships. The best consumer-goods companies should know more about their consumers and their categories than any private-label manufacturer. Indeed, they should also know more than their trade customers, who, though closer to the end consumer and inundated with scanner purchase data, have to plan assortments of products and allocate shelf space for 250 to 300 categories with only the resources that 1% after-tax profit margins will permit. Manufacturers must leverage their knowledge to create a win-win proposition for their trade accounts: Retailers and national-brand producers can maximize their profits jointly without excessive emphasis on private labels. They can do so if manufacturers take these steps:

- Loan retailers an accountant to educate them about private-label profitability. A *Brandweek* survey reported that 88% of retailers believe private labels can increase category profits whereas only 31% of manufacturers believe this. Many retailers emphasize private-label products because they often deliver a higher percentage of profit margins than national brands. However, the rate of private-label turnover and the absolute dollar margin per unit may be lower. In addition, retailers often mistakenly compare apples and oranges. They don't always take account of promotion costs for the store name that builds

private-label demand. They also may omit their ware-
housing and distribution costs for private-label products when comparing private-label retail margins
with those of national brands that manufacturers
deliver direct to stores and stock on the shelves.

- Offer to examine retailers' purchase scanner data.
  Invariably, the shopper who buys a national brand
  rather than the private label in the same category
  spends more per supermarket visit and delivers a
  higher absolute and percentage margin to the retailer.
  The private-label shopper is not the most profitable
  for the retailer.

- Subsidize in-store experiments. Retailers' views of
  how many consumers are attracted to their stores by
  private labels is often exaggerated. National-brand
  manufacturers can suggest and pay for tests that
  compare the sales and profitability of a control store's
  current shelf-space allocation plan with the sales and
  profitability of a shelf-space plan offering fewer or no
  private-label goods.

- Ration support. By responding to customers and
  managing categories more efficiently, leading manufacturers have found new ways of favoring trade
  accounts that support their national brands over private labels and of not being quite so helpful to those
  that don't. For example, companies are becoming
  increasingly sophisticated about how they spend
  their trade dollars. Instead of giving straight discounts, manufacturers are asking for "pay for performance," in which retailers are paid more if their sales
  activities are successful.

Manage the price spread. During the 1980s, consumer goods manufacturers increased prices ahead of inflation (the easiest way to add bottom-line profit in the short term) and then offered periodic reductions off their artificially inflated list prices to distributors and consumers who demanded them. As long as some still paid full price, this price discrimination was thought to be profitable. Over time, however, such a high proportion of the typical brand's volume was being sold at a deep discount that the list prices no longer had credibility. Further, the added manufacturing and logistics costs of the promotions and the increased price sensitivity they stimulated played into the hands of private labels. When Marlboro cut its list prices, it correspondingly reduced the level and frequency of its promotions; the list price was restored to a more credible level while the hidden costs from the brand's use of promotions were reduced.

Brand-name manufacturers must leverage their knowledge of consumers and categories to benefit their trade accounts.

National-brand manufacturers must monitor the price gap both to the distributor and to the end consumer between each national brand and the other brands, including private labels, in every market. They must also understand how elastic the price is for each national brand—that is, how much effect changes in price have on consumers. For example, a 5% increase over the private-label price in the price premium of a sample national brand may result in a 2% loss of share. But an increase of 10% may result in an additional 3%

loss. With an increase between 10% and 15%, only 2% more might be lost because the remaining national-brand customers are now the less-price-sensitive loyals. (See Stephen J. Hoch and Shumeet Bannerji, "When Do Private Labels Succeed?" *Sloan Management Review,* Summer 1993, pp. 57–67.)

Knowing the shape of your brand's price elasticity curve is essential to smart pricing and to maximizing the brand's profitability. A price reduction on a popular national brand may result in a lower profit contribution, but studies show that private-label sales are twice as sensitive as national brands to changes in the price gap. In other words, a decrease in the price gap would swing twice as many sales from private labels to national brands as a corresponding increase would swing sales to private labels from national brands. (See the graph "Price Elasticity of National Brands.")

Exploit sales-promotion tactics. National-brand manufacturers cannot prevent retailers from displaying copycat private-label products alongside their brands with "compare and save" signs heralding the price gaps. However, they can use sales promotion tactics to enhance the merchandising of their brands. Strong brands with full product lines such as Neutrogena can sometimes secure retail space for their own custom-built displays. Manufacturers can emphasize performance-based merchandising allowances that require special in-store displays or advertisements over cash discounts applied to invoices. They can reward retailers for increasing sales volume (as verified by scanner records) with rebates. And they can distribute coupons to households in areas where retailers are aggressively providing private-label products.

Manage each category. What works for detergents won't necessarily work for soft drinks. Categories differ widely in private-label penetration, the price-quality gap between private labels and national brands, and the relative profitability and potential cannibalization cost of any private label or value brand.

- In categories with low private-label penetration such as candy and baby food, managers must understand and sustain the barriers to entry—such as frequent technological improvements within a category, a

---

Price Elasticity of National Brands

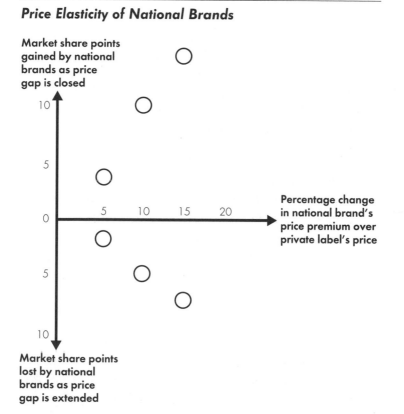

manufacturer's low-cost producer status, or intense competition among national brands. In one case, an easy-to-prepare dinner entree had seen modest private-label sales for years, but sales exploded once private-label manufacturers acquired the technology for an increasingly popular form of the product.

- In categories with emerging private-label penetration, it is useful to consider value-added packaging changes—and, in some circumstances, line extensions—that make the product stand out on the shelf, keep consumers' attention focused on the national brands, and raise the costs for private-label imitators. In part, we have private-label pressure to thank for easy-open and resealable packages. Promotions targeted at trade accounts showing interest in private labels may also be useful, along with advertising (such as the 1994 "Nothing Else is a Pepsi" campaign) that focuses consumers on the advantages of the national brand and then warns them against imitations.

- In categories with well-established private-label penetration, the goal is containment. The emphasis must be on lowering the costs in the supply chain—through minimum orders, truckload and direct shipment discounts, more efficient trade deals, and the elimination of slow-moving stockkeeping units—to save money for reinvestment in the brand.

Use category profit pools as a performance measure. Most consumer-goods companies use market share and volume as the primary measurement tools for category performance. These tools can lead to poor decision making because they inherently value all share points equally. Consumer Corporation, as part of its effort to manage the profitability of its marketing, tracked and analyzed the profit pool for all its categories. That is, it calculated the total profit for all participants in a category by segment and then attributed percentages of the total to the companies competing within that category. Not surprisingly, low-volume, low-profit private labels appear to be far less important when using this measurement. When a manufacturer's objectives are to maximize both the overall category profit pool and its share of that pool, the decision making is generally very different from traditional share and volume measures.

Take private labels seriously. Too many national brands treat private-label competition as an afterthought in their annual marketing plans. They regard only the other national brands as their true competitors. The emergence of premium private labels and national store brands such as Sam's makes this oversight more and more dangerous. Stealing market share from weaker national brands often merely opens the door for more serious private-label competition. Every national-brand marketing plan should include a section on how to limit the encroachment of private labels. The marketing plan might include specific actions to be taken in categories, trade accounts, or regional markets where reports indicate private labels are gaining ground. In addition, national-brand manufacturers should bring more legal actions against copycat private labelers who use the same packaging shapes and colors as the national brands, and they should tighten arrangements with contract suppliers to prevent them from using new proprietary technologies in the manufacture of private-label products.

N ATIONAL-BRAND MANUFACTURERS can use some or all of the strategies outlined above to win the battle against private-label producers. Consider the results of the Coca-Cola Company's response to Cott in Canada, where the market for private-label soft drink sales was strong. After Coca-Cola retaliated aggressively against Cott in 1994, the latter's profits as a percentage of sales plummeted along with its stock price; the company then moderated its ambitions to extend its private-label success formula to other product categories. Cott executives stated that the company's growth would thereafter come as a result of overall market expansion and at the expense of competitors smaller than Coca-Cola. By taking firm, considered action, brand-name manufacturers can successfully fight the private-label challenge.

What Drives Private-Label Shares?

The percentage of units accounted for by private labels varies widely by category. To some degree, the variation is a function of time—private-label canned foods, for example, have been on the market longer and in broader distribution than private-label diapers. However, researchers have identified several factors, listed below, that favor private-label penetration.

Product category characteristics:

- The product is an inexpensive, easy, low-risk purchase for the consumer.

- It is easy to make from commodity ingredients.

- It is perishable, thereby favoring local suppliers.

- Product category sales are large and growing, so private labels can more easily garner sufficient volume to be profitable.

- The category is dominated by a few national-brand manufacturers, so retailers promote private labels to reduce dependency on them.

New-product activity:

- National brands are offered in few varieties, enabling a private label with a narrow line to represent a clear alternative to the consumer.

- National-brand new-product introductions are infrequent or easy to copy.

- Consumers can easily make side-by-side comparisons of national brands and private labels.

Private-label characteristics:

- Private-label goods have been available to consumers for many years.

- Distribution is well developed.

- Variability in quality is low.

- Quality in comparison with national brands is high and improving.

- Consumers have confidence in their ability to make comparisons about quality.

Price and promotion factors:

- Retail gross margins in the product category are relatively high.

- Price gaps between national brands and private labels are wide.

- National-brand expenditures on price promotions as a percentage of sales are high, raising price sensitivity and encouraging consumers to switch brands.

- The credibility of national-brand prices is low because of frequent and deep price promotions.

- National-brand expenditures on advertising as a percentage of sales are low.

Retailer characteristics:

- The retailer is part of a stable oligopoly and therefore sells national brands at relatively high prices.

- The retailer has the size and resources to invest in high-quality private-label development.

Originally published in January–February 1996
Reprint 96109

How Do You Grow a Premium Brand?

REGINA FAZIO MARUCA

Executive Summary

GORDON JOHNSTON HAS TAKEN his elite health-club concept form the germ of an idea to the pinnacle of success. But the most difficult decision in managing this company lies ahead. Gordon must figure out how to lead Transition fitness clubs into the next phase.

In each of the 15 years since Transition's flagship club opened in New York City, its sales have doubled. What the company calls a "two-hour miracle" encompasses fitness trainers handpicked by Olympic medalists, health-conscious cuisine by in-house chefs, huge facilities in prime locations, and reciprocal memberships at other Transition clubs worldwide.

But recently, the company's margins have been shrinking. An aging membership could mean problems for future expansion. And new, upscale competitors are challenging Transition's pricing policy—a high flat rate that includes everything—with prorated packages tailored to clients' needs.

Transition is also facing competition on another level. For the past ten years, the company has offered its services through satellite clubs in the prestigious Printemps hotels. Now Printemps's main competitor, the Clarkhouse chain, offers similar fitness facilities. Clarkhouse has 250 locations worldwide, Printemps only 35.

What can Gordon do? His staff is alarmed that he is considering overtures from the midpriced Ambassador hotel chain. They think he will risk Transition's reputation by offering a downscale version of the club.

Will Gordon have to run fast to stay in one place? Should he change Transition's pricing policy? Six experts in marketing, pricing, and product branding advise Gordon on how to transition Transition.

I T WAS A GREAT IDEA. The first of its kind. A series of ultrapremium health clubs located in major cities throughout the world. Targeted at senior executives too busy to eat. Frequent business travelers. Singles. People who just plain liked the extra attention and pampering and could afford to pay for the best.

And it really had taken off. Since its flagship club had opened at one of New York City's most prestigious addresses 15 years ago, Transition's sales had doubled each year. The first location, a 25,000-square-foot facility with 14 full-time staff members, plus numerous sales associates, was almost maxed out at 2,300 members. Within its first two years of operation, Transition had opened similarly popular facilities in other major cities: Chicago, Washington, Los Angeles, London, Paris, Milan, Singapore, Hong Kong, and Tokyo. Within five years, it was also operating through the five-star Printemps hotels, offering its services to guests.

It wasn't just clever marketing. True, the initial campaign—a targeted direct-mail effort featuring an endorsement from four-time Wimbledon winner Julia Sonoma—had generated a solid response. And Transition advertised regularly in publications such as the *New York Times, Town and Country*, and the *London Times*. But word of mouth also had served the company well. Transition was elite—offering top-of-the-line services to a select clientele—and its reputation had spread quickly throughout the ranks of wealthy jet-setters and business travelers. Early on, it had developed a reputation as the Tiffany of health clubs. And its name became known worldwide as the best of the best.

Despite the success, however, owner and president Gordon Johnston was feeling unsettled. Transition's margins were shrinking. In the past 12 months, sales growth had flattened, while operating expenses had continued to rise. Gordon had to pay a premium for celebrity chefs and former Olympic coaches and athletes. His staff-to-member ratio was high compared with most other clubs. And he had deliberately created high-cost facilities, asking his architect to survey the top health clubs in each Transition city and then to design spaces that were 30% larger than the existing highest standard. Maintaining such plush facilities in prime locations wasn't what anyone would call cheap.

What's more, the club's niche suddenly seemed precarious. Market share was difficult to track, but Gordon's sense was that the number of companies entering the high-end health club and spa scene was growing fast, even though Transition had stalled. To top it off, Transition's membership was aging. The average member age was now 46; ten years ago, it had been 41.

Gordon, a former senior executive at Moira Point, an exclusive California golf club, was in his large, modern office at Transition's Chicago facility. From his desk, he could see through a one-way mirror into the weight room. He leaned back in his chair and watched his business working. The Nautilus circuit was busy but not too crowded, and seven of the eight step machines were also in use. Not bad, given that it was already 8 P.M. on a Thursday night.

He thought about the competition and told himself to calm down. Technically, Transition didn't have competition. It was an elite organization: the only one of its kind. He took a deep breath and picked up his copy of the *Wall Street Journal*, but almost immediately, he could feel his blood pressure rise again. There, on page 9, was a full-page ad for the Fitworth health club chain. Manhattan-based Fitworth was one of the successful recent start-ups, and the company's new campaign was clearly an attack on Transition.

"Sure, you can afford it, but why pay for something you don't use?" was the slogan—a direct shot at Transition's all-inclusive, one-price membership plan. Transition charged a $600 initiation fee, plus $2,300 per year for a membership. Food and beverages were extra— available at prices comparable to finer casual restaurants in New York City. Fitworth charged an $800 initiation but, after that, the yearly membership fee depended on which of a large variety of service packages the individual member chose. For example, a $1,000 yearly fee included unlimited use of facilities, with an additional hourly charge for staff assistance. A $1,500 yearly fee included access to the facilities, training staff, and massage therapists. Fitworth did not provide in-house chefs. But it did offer a limited dinner menu using reputable area caterers on a pay-as-you-go basis, at a cost of about 20% less than Transition's. And although it didn't occupy superprime locations like Transition's, it had managed to open facilities within walking distance of twelve of Transition's clubs in the United States. Fitworth had also set up a reciprocal-membership alliance with Japan's Mind and Body spas, which had facilities throughout the Asia-Pacific region, and with England's True Worth clubs.

Gordon resigned himself to his tense mood and mentally reviewed the situation. Besides Fitworth, he was worried about Clarkhouse, a top-rated hotel chain that had recently opened its own line of health clubs. True, Clarkhouse was not in quite the same league as Printemps, but it had one clear advantage: whereas Printemps had only 35 locations worldwide, Clarkhouse had more than 250. Whenever the regular clientele of Printemps visited cities without a Printemps hotel, most turned to Clarkhouse.

Gordon left his office and walked down the hall to get a drink of water. There was yet another issue on his mind. A midprice Los Angeles-based hotel group, the Ambassador hotels, had approached him with a proposal to carry the Transition clubs at its locations worldwide. Expanding was an exciting prospect, and Ambassador was a well-respected international chain. But it wasn't anywhere near the top of the line, like Printemps or Clarkhouse. Working with Ambassador would mean expanding not only Transition's reach but also its target market. Would that work? And how would the Printemps management react to the alliance?

Since its flagship club opened 15 years ago, sales had doubled yearly.

Returning to his comfortable office, Gordon sat down
at his computer. He began to type out his thoughts. He
would fax them to Scott Conner, his director of sales and
marketing, and get his feedback.

Friday night, almost 10:30 P.M. It was time for Transition's flagship facility to shut its doors for the night. But
Scott Conner was still on the phone with Gordon, trying
to make some sense of the new plan for expansion and
pricing that Gordon had faxed to him early that morning. He'd been on this call for almost two hours, and he
was more confused and dismayed now than he'd been at
the outset.

"Our whole philosophy is based on the notion that
we're a unique premium offering," Scott said, acknowl-
edging a knock at the door with a nod and waving Kim
Cole, the company's number one sales associate, into a
seat. "Our sales staff has been trained to position this
health club as a top-of-the-line product: one price covers
everything. We can't offer less; we can't sell less. When we
talk to prospective members, we implicitly *put down* the
other kinds of clubs and spas—sometimes we even do it
directly. You're undermining the core strategy here, and
if we do it your way, we'll be cutting our own throats."

Scott was quiet for a few moments, then spoke again.
"No, I completely oppose this. You can't trade off our
reputation like that. We'll be just like everyone else. I
don't . . . Well, we'll just have to . . . Can I just say
one thing?" He was silent again. Kim rolled her eyes.

"Fine, we'll meet on Tuesday at 3. Chicago. Yes." He
hung up, then mustered a small smile for Kim. "Well, as
you can see, Gordon isn't going to let this new idea of his
die without a fight."

Kim knew about Gordon's plan. Scott had shared the
initial memo with her that morning, and she, too, had

been incredulous. But she was also pragmatic. "If he's convinced, there's really nothing you can do about it," she said, shrugging. "It's his company. And maybe he's right. You're just coming at this from the sales perspective. Gordon is thinking of the company as a whole."

"But it can't work his way." Scott got out of his chair and grabbed his jacket off the coatrack. "Let's round up Frank and get out of here."

Frank Casale, Transition's director of operations and facilities, was in his office working on domestic budgets. "It's about time," he said, as Scott and Kim appeared at his door. He shut down his computer and grabbed his jacket.

Frank, Scott, and Kim had a standing meeting every Friday night after work. Their long hours precluded any kind of normal Friday night socializing with their families or friends, so the trio generally went to a small restaurant and bar downtown to eat their artery-clogging meat-and-potatoes meal and just unwind. There was a rule: nothing said at dinner left the table. And generally the meals were fun; there was a lot of teasing and laughter about the week's events. But tonight was a different story.

First, Scott and Kim brought Frank up to date on the memo; then Scott rehashed his conversation with Gordon.

Frank listened quietly as he ate. But when Scott said, "I tell you, Gordon has lost his mind," for the third time, Frank spoke up.

"I hate to be the one to burst your bubble, Scott, but Gordon has a really good idea here. I mean, we might be the top of the line right now, but we do charge more than anyone else, and our target market is limited. I do what I can to manage costs, but if we don't grow, it'll be a real squeeze. The budget keeps growing, and the only way I can maintain quality facilities is if we grow revenues. Only a certain group of people is ever going to use a Transition club. Gordon is an entrepreneur, and I agree with him that it's time to find a way to expand, or at least broaden our niche."

He took a drink of beer and continued quickly before Scott could start up again. "You said Gordon proposes that we drop our annual fee and instead charge a high, one-time initiation fee with a corporate discount and package pricing for various services. He's done the math; the projections look solid to him. What's wrong with that? At least a third of our members don't use the full club anyway. Who wants to pay for a massage they never get, regardless of their income? And what's wrong with using the Transition name at Ambassador hotels? That's expansion. You know we don't have anyplace to expand at the top: why not go down a notch?"

Lately margins were shrinking: the club's niche now seemed precarious.

"Would Tiffany sell a cheap line of jewelry at a department store boutique?" Kim cut in. "Can't you see? We'll lose our marketing edge."

"Not if it's done properly," Frank countered. He turned to Scott. "When are you going to meet with Gordon about this? I think you should tell him what you think, but keep an open mind."

Monday morning, 7:30 A.M. Gordon finished reading Scott's five-page memo for the third time and then got up to get another glass of orange juice from the club's kitchen. He thought Scott had valid concerns, but he knew that he didn't need Scott's approval to make a decision. He also knew that he didn't have to make any decision right away. He had calmed down since Thursday. In fact, if he put off making a move now, he could explore another idea: opening Transition satellite spas at certain corporate headquarters. Really, the possibilities were endless.

Can Transition Expand without Losing Its Elite Aura?

Six experts consider the options.

WILLIAM CAMPBELL *is the chairman of Philip Morris U.S.A.*

Yes, Gordon Johnston should take action. But he should first think about which of his current alternatives are high risk and which are low risk and then consider each option against his management capability as it presently stands.

Take pricing. I'm probably known as the world's greatest price dropper. Marlboro Friday had a tremendous impact. But changing a pricing policy is an extremely high-risk maneuver. If Gordon rolls out a pricing change without proper testing, he could completely lose Transition's image, and he might never gain the kind of volume he would need to make up the loss.

Considering the skills of Gordon's existing staff, however, a pricing option might be a good place to start. Right now, Transition's top staff and management talent seems to be almost exclusively sales oriented. For that reason, I might start by having them explore some price discounting options, but in a very limited context. Scott Conner and his group should select the most isolated Transition location—definitely *not* downtown New York or Chicago—and experiment there. That way, if they find that different pricing policies confuse or alienate current customers, the damage is limited. Remember, Transition's customers believe that the club's high price and high quality together create value. As soon as the company starts tampering with the price, it's telling customers that they have gotten bad value in the past.

One experiment might be corporate membership plans targeted at organizations that wouldn't be candidates for their own satellite clubs later on. That's an area in which a discount wouldn't significantly alter Transition's image. Scott could also try limited promotional efforts to see how customers react. A corporate membership plan is the kind of product that could benefit tremendously from good use of selective mailing lists. But again, Scott should experiment in an isolated, quiet way. This can be done in the health club business—in *our* business, it's difficult to do anything quietly.

All the pricing tests should be slow and thorough. And even if they have excellent results, Transition should drop or alter its price companywide only after every other alternative has been examined. We tried other alternatives for two years—while testing pricing in isolated markets—before implementing Marlboro's new price across the board. The Marlboro pricing action was ultimately very successful, as our test markets predicted.

While Scott and his crew are experimenting with price in this limited fashion, Gordon might turn his own attention to something we at Philip Morris call a *flanker* strategy: launching a new line of products with a certain limited association to the parent brand.

For example, he could start a line of clubs called Profiles by Transition and trim the new product back approximately in proportion to its price. If he openly takes something out of the product—the gourmet food, for example—that would allow him to defend to past club members the new, lower price, and if he makes it clear that the product is not simply a lesser version of the original but something unique in its own right, he can succeed.

A flanker strategy is a lower-risk option than a pricing change, but eventually a move like that would require additional management skills. Gordon could start out in a limited way. He could use the strategy to explore the Ambassador hotel offer—maybe by seeing if Ambassador will open two or three Profiles clubs to test the market. Gordon can also run a test in a few freestanding locations. Maybe the Profiles by Transition clubs could start out in the lake suburbs near Chicago and in Ambassador hotels in a few other suburban areas. In hotels and in suburbs near the members' homes, Transition's meal service would be irrelevant. There's a good opportunity to unload a huge cost base and come in as a midprice entry without affecting the quality image.

Here, as with the pricing experiments, I would try to stay as far away from a Transition hub as possible. Gordon doesn't want his current membership to feel as though they're overpaying for a similar product. At the same time, he should try to ensure that he doesn't go so far away that the Transition name loses its positive rub-off.

Gordon's lowest-risk alternative seems to be the corporate satellite plan. That kind of product will never be compared head-on with his existing business, but, as he opens corporate health clubs, he will be able to take advantage of Transition's excellent reputation and its superior image. The satellite clubs would be a

custom-designed business that I think Gordon would
be very good at.

That option, however, definitely requires a larger
management team. Perhaps as he is exploring the
flanker strategy, Gordon can build a staff that is able to
handle the corporate satellite idea—assuming, of course,
that he is somewhat financially secure and willing to
invest the funds.

Gordon has a solid position in a growth industry. He
has several good opportunities before him, and, if he
moves carefully, he can begin to segment the market
and participate in growth without endangering his core
franchise.

ROBERT J. DOLAN *is the Edward W. Carter Professor of
Business Administration at the Harvard Business School
in Boston, Massachusetts, where he teaches the advanced
management program. His most recent book is* Managing the New Product Development Process *(Addison-Wesley, 1993).*

Gordon Johnston is looking in the wrong place for a
solution to his problem. Like all businesses, Transition
faces consumers who are increasingly value conscious.
That and the emergence of credible competition have
created growth and margin pressures that warrant a
response. But destroying the Transition message is not
the answer. And that is precisely what Gordon would do
by trading down the ultrapremium Transition brand
with a switch to à la carte pricing and an association
with Ambassador.

Consider the pricing policy changes Gordon has proposed. Right now, he has the most simple pricing
scheme possible—pay $2,300 a year, and use what you
want. He's worried about Fitworth's attack: "Sure, you

can afford it, but why pay for something you don't use?" Fitworth's campaign, however, misses an important fact: Transition's current method allows members to focus on benefits, not on a series of costs.

Gordon's dilemma reminds me of a country club that had a similar pricing policy. You would pay a membership fee of $2,300 per year, play the course as often as you wanted, practice as much as you wanted on the driving range, get a permanent storage locker with towels as needed, and store your clubs at the pro shop. Thus you'd pay once, then forget about it and enjoy yourself.

A handful of vocal members noted the obvious fact that some people used the club a lot more than others, some had homes adjacent to the course and didn't need a locker, and some played at lots of other courses and liked to store their clubs in their cars. So the management rolled out a new pricing plan, which they felt had to be better than the old one because members could still do just what they always did, while enjoying some new options. Specifically, members could follow the Fitworth philosophy and pay only for services they used: $1,800 a year to play as much as they wanted, plus a variety of special offerings (driving range privileges, $200; locker and towel service, $200; club storage and daily cleaning, $100).

The plan looked good on paper. Management hoped members would say to themselves, "If I buy the whole package for $1,800 plus $200 plus $200 plus $100, the total is $2,300, so I am at least as well off as before." More options are always better, right?

Wrong. Members instead began to be cost conscious. "Let's see. I play Saturdays and Sundays in June, July, and August, plus five straight days when I take vacation, plus maybe once or twice in September—so that's about

30 times a year. Half the time, I just make my tee time, so I don't hit more than a handful of balls at the range before going out to play. So I certainly don't hit many balls on more than 20 occasions per year. If I pay the $200 annual fee, that's $10 each time. I guess it isn't really worth it for me. But most days, I do like to hit a couple of balls. Boy, they're really taking advantage of me here. I could buy new balls and hit them into the woods and spend less than $200 a year. How can it cost twice as much to hit a few balls as it costs to have your clubs stored? Why can't they just let me buy a bucket of balls when I want to? Now, if I pay the $200 for range privileges, every time I come here I'll be running over there to hit balls whether I want to or not; otherwise, I won't get my $200 worth."

The new pricing plan reduced most members' overall enjoyment of the facility because it brought cost into their minds every time they entered the club grounds. That's why the new pricing plan lasted only one season. If the club's managers hadn't scrapped it, they would have ruined the business.

Like the golf club's original pricing plan, Transition's current policy succeeds because it minimizes complicated cost/benefit calculations. Members are not distracted by trade-offs, nor do they have to make any compromises to enjoy the club. The policy is an integral part of the product-service offering and a key to providing value to the customer. Changing it would pull the rug out from under the all-inclusive, top-of-the-line platform on which Transition's success rests.

Similarly, the Transition name does not belong with the "midprice" and "well-respected" Ambassador hotels. Scott Conner is right: Transition's philosophy is based on the notion that it is a "unique premium offering." As such, its growth opportunities may in fact be limited. But that's OK. It is a natural result of the focus and clarity of Transition in meeting the needs of a select group. As Frank Casale notes, "Only a certain group of people is ever going to use a Transition club." It ought to stay that way. Growth avenues for the company are available elsewhere if the geographic scope of Transition has already been maximized.

Gordon's organization can grow its revenues by working with Ambassador to create an additional club concept, meeting and exceeding requirements of consumers whose demands are not as extensive as those of Transition members. The offspring club should not be called Transition—but through its marketing efforts, Gordon and Ambassador can make sure that the target market understands that the talent behind Transition's customer-satisfying efforts is equally committed to success with the new concept.

A move to serve the mid-to-upper-level tier, as opposed to just the ultrapremium tier, would place Gordon in a more intensely competitive market. However, the skills his organization has developed in creating and operating the Transition franchise will enable it to build a high-quality, differentiated offering here as well. Gordon must simply remember that quality is not based on gold-medalist-selected trainers, prize-winning architecture, free massages, or 30% more space between treadmills—unless that's what his target market is really seeking. A high-quality product meets and exceeds the requirements of customers at a price they are willing to pay. High quality may be defined differently by different groups.

Gordon can marshal the talents he has on hand to develop a new club he's proud of and one that generates

the revenues he's seeking. And the new endeavor may
keep him from the danger that he is now flirting with—
piecemeal changes to Transition that in the end would
destroy it.

ANITA K. HERSH *is president and COO of the New York
City–based consulting firm Lister Butler, which provides
strategic corporate- and brand-identity counsel to U.S.
and international companies.*

Gordon must manage his business to meet the changing needs and expectations of consumers. Recognizing
some significant changes in the health club business, he
is appropriately concerned about the future growth and
success of Transition and should explore alternative strategies. He is in a good position to do so.
In the course of creating a successful business,
Gordon has built up a solid and respected brand. The
Transition brand is an asset with significant value and
equity and can be leveraged to extend the company into
new markets, products, or services.

The Transition brand will be both more valuable and more at risk if it's called on to do more work.

Almost any of the ideas that Gordon is considering is
worth exploring. Each would take Transition beyond the
limited niche market it now occupies. That said, however, Gordon must understand that the Transition
brand will become both more valuable and more at risk
as he asks it to do more work. To protect it, he should
keep one thing first and foremost in his mind: a key
component of any business strategy he pursues is his
brand identity strategy. The brand's identity system is
the most essential vehicle for communicating what the
company, product, or service is. This system (brand

names and nomenclature, logotypes and symbols, colors, corporate voice, and visual style) embodies the meaning of the brand—what it stands for and what it has to offer. Any innovative strategy for changing or for expanding the business must address the need to protect the core Transition brand while using it to win new customers and extend its reach into new markets.

For example, consider the possibility of extending downmarket. Sheraton Hotels pursued a strategy to leverage its core brand by introducing Sheraton Inn to appeal to more value-conscious travelers. Similarly, in 1994, Mercedes-Benz successfully introduced its C-Class line of automobiles to capture the lower end of the luxury car market. The value of the Mercedes brand clearly had a lot to do with the success of the C-Class line. Mercedes leveraged the core values and attributes of the brand—engineering superiority, reliability, and service— to develop the C-Class line but did not undermine the positioning of its high-end E- and S-Class lines. Transition could consider a similar downmarket strategy.

Or Gordon could decide to remain in the elite market niche he currently occupies and expand the business at that level. A strong brand identity can be a significant aid to selling new and related products—look at how successfully Porsche has introduced Porsche-brand eyewear and precision timepieces.

One thing that might help Gordon as he evaluates options is to think of the brand as a promise—a promise of certain attributes and values from the supplier, a promise of quality, a promise of performance, and a promise of a certain level of service. What is the Transition brand promise? What does the Transition brand stand for? The answers will provide a basis for determining where the brand name and visual identity should be used, and it will ensure that it isn't used on something that will hurt the brand and the business.

As Gordon moves forward in developing and implementing his new business plans, he needs to do so judiciously, recognizing that there are systematic approaches to managing brand identity just as for any other significant business asset. He should try to manage Transition's brand identity as carefully as its other functions, from finance to the quality of services. By exercising a great deal of care and respecting what the brand means, he can protect and expand brand value.

PETER H. FARQUHAR *is a professor of management at the Peter F. Drucker Graduate Management Center in Claremont, California. He is also director of the Product Strategy Institute at the Claremont Graduate School.*

Gordon's most promising opportunity may be the idea he introduced at the very end of the case: opening satellite Transition spas at select corporate headquarters. But before he takes any action, he should step back and assess the situation as a whole. The dangers he senses in the marketplace are real, and, if he addresses one but ignores another, the Transition brand could suffer irrevocable damage. At the same time, however, reacting to every perceived threat without thinking through the consequences won't help: some of Gordon's proposed responses are way off the mark.

For starters, he should take a hard look at the new line of Clarkhouse health clubs. These pose a serious threat to Transition. Our field research at the Drucker Management Center shows that incumbents are often displaced by challengers that create alternate channels of distribution for their brands and appeal to new customers. Eventually, the emerging brand leaders begin to attract customers from traditional channels, and then the old leader is in trouble.

Clarkhouse's 250 hotels easily dwarf Transition's presence in the 35 Printemps locations. Since Printemps hotels' regular clients use Clarkhouse hotels in many locations, Clarkhouse has a remarkable opportunity to convert Transition's customers. Much of what is commonly regarded as brand equity is really strength in distribution.

What's more, Gordon's cobranding alliance with Printemps hotels puts Transition in a competitively weak position to defend its brand. Business travelers will mentally credit Printemps rather than Transition for their hotel health club experiences. Clarkhouse, meanwhile, will be using its strong reputation to great advantage. Since the club and the hotel chain are one name and one brand, Clarkhouse will easily be able to transfer its brand equity to its new offering.

Less critical than the Clarkhouse threat but still a serious problem is Transition's own image-building strategy—or lack thereof. Incumbent leaders are also vulnerable to challengers like Fitworth that customize their brand offerings to provide a more convenient or valued mix of services for individual customers. Transition's flattened sales growth and aging membership are telltale signs that its service mix has fallen behind the changing needs of the marketplace. How many people do you know today who want to take time for a gourmet dinner after a workout and a massage? Transition must rejuvenate the brand or else risk becoming a has-been in the fast-paced world of health and fitness.

Scott Conner seems to advocate a "stick-to-your-knitting" brand strategy. He maintains that Transition is a "unique premium offering" and recommends continued positioning as "an all-inclusive, top-of-the-line product." That's fine, as long as continued positioning doesn't also mean stagnation. The success of his proposed strategy rests on two key conditions: Transition's service differentiation must remain both relevant and important to customers, and Transition's perceived service quality must be decisively better than anything offered by others in the market. By attracting Transition's clients with a customized service mix and unbundled prices, chains such as Fitworth provide evidence that Transition's service differentiation may be less relevant or less decisive an advantage than it once was. The playing field is nearly level in many customers' minds.

Opening corporate satellite clubs is probably his most promising option. Certain companies would have a huge market potential.

One brand renewal strategy Transition might try is leapfrogging competitive offerings with truly innovative services that anticipate latent customer needs or satisfy existing needs in a significantly better way. (That, of course, was the company's strategy when it first entered the market 15 years ago.) Transition's signature services—such as coaches chosen by Olympians, celebrity chefs, elegant club decor, and prestigious locations—have probably grown old with many customers. Gordon should ask Frank, Scott, and Kim to refocus efforts on the development of fresh, new client services—breakthrough ideas—that will revitalize Transition's brand image and strengthen its customer base.

Opening corporate satellite clubs is probably Gordon's most promising option. He could use Transition's good name to develop such alternate channels of distribution, which may in turn reinforce his established channels. Certain corporations would have a huge market potential and represent a relatively captive market. That sounds like a "reemerging brand leader" strategy Gordon should explore.

If he doesn't want to go that route, he can try to grow the company through some sort of alliance with Ambassador hotels, but Gordon shouldn't cobrand the Transition name with Ambassador. Transition's reputation would be diluted in such a relationship (although Ambassador would receive a boost), and the alliance with Printemps would probably fall apart. Cobranding generally works for both parties only when the two brands are approximately equal in strength for the same target customers.

If the growth opportunity is attractive enough, Gordon might focus instead on leveraging his company reputation by building a bridge brand—that is, by creating a separate new brand name for the Transition/Ambassador offering. He could use the Transition brand to endorse the new bridge brand (which he might call, for example, "Wellfleet from Transition") to gain initial trial and to speed acceptance in the marketplace. Or he might consider an endorsement that would compete with Clarkhouse, such as "Wellfleet by Ambassador." Brand association maps and other marketing research measures could help determine the optimal course here. Then, once the new brand gained sufficient strength, the endorsement could fade from view as appropriate.

A bridge strategy would establish a more suitable partner for Gordon to use with Ambassador than the elite Transition brand. (Using this strategy, Gordon might also approach other, similar hotels on a nonexclusive basis.) A bridge strategy would protect the

Transition brand from dilution, while allowing the company to expand.

DAVID A. AAKER *is the E.T. Grether Chair of Marketing and Public Policy at the Walter A. Haas School of Business Administration, University of California at Berkeley. He is the author of* Managing Brand Equity *(Free Press, 1991).*

Associating with a lesser hotel chain like Ambassador could damage the Transition brand irrevocably by tarnishing the prestige and perceived quality that is the core of its brand equity. Such a partnership would dilute the Transition identity in general and severely strain the credibility of the Printemps operations. Gordon should search for an alternative that builds on the asset of prestige. He might try enhancing the company's service offering. Or, if he really wants (or needs) the company to grow, he could introduce horizontal product extensions. Both of these ideas could be accomplished within Transition's current market for its current clientele.

Enhancing the service offering (perhaps also making a small downward adjustment in pricing) would raise the bar for competitors. Transition would no longer be a stationary target. And creative people can always find ways to improve service without major increases in cost. Perhaps Transition's team could introduce a set of fruit drinks with interesting labels. Or Transition could simply package some existing services under a new umbrella—for example, a personal development program—that would enhance the value proposition.

Horizontal product extensions might include travel planning for active, exotic vacations. Or the club could market exercise equipment and accessories, either on site or through a catalog. Gordon could use alternatives like these to reinforce the brand's identity and help his company grow.

Suppose, however, an analysis suggests that Transition's current market—even with additional service and product offerings—is not large enough to sustain profitability over the long term, despite the company's prestigious brand name. Suppose further that the analysis reveals profitable growth areas outside the very high end that Transition has staked out. How can an established premium brand participate in the trend while minimizing risks? It's not impossible. Gordon can successfully develop a new kind of club and make a clean, profitable, downscale move, but he should develop his concept first and then, if he still thinks an alliance is a good idea, look for partners.

Courtyard by Marriott, Kodak Funtime, and Gillette Good News are notable examples of successful downscaling.

Courtyard by Marriott hotels, Kodak Funtime film, and Gillette Good News disposable razors are examples of successful downscaling. These ventures and others like them suggest four guidelines for Transition's expansion into a broader market.

- Gordon should make sure that the club's downscale version is qualitatively different from Transition, not simply an inferior replica. It can be distinguished by color scheme, ambience, background music, services, or location. Courtyard, for example, is clearly distinct from Marriott: it has fewer services and offers a different hotel experience.

- The new offering should be aimed at a market that does not overlap with Gordon's current target. That will reduce the risk of confusion among current Transition clientele. There's less danger that the original brand image will be tarnished if the original market is not likely to hear about the new offering. The downscale club could be targeted toward a younger clientele, for example, or toward people in smaller cities.

- A sub-brand should be used to help distinguish the new offering from the other products that are under the umbrella of the parent brand. The sub-brands Courtyard, Funtime, and Good News partially insulate their parent brands by providing their own distinct identities. In a lab study at Berkeley that I conducted recently with doctoral student Steve Markey, we found that damage to a major brand of tissues and to a popular fruit drink line from the introduction of inferior extensions (a hard, coarse toilet paper and a watery orange juice) would be sharply reduced if the extensions were presented to consumers as sub-brands.

- Gordon should create a brand personality for the new offering that is distinct from Transition's personality. He might try establishing a parent-child kind of relationship between the two. The typical Transition member might be an older person with wealth, professional success, and social prestige; and the profile of the offspring member could be of someone much younger with a lot of energy and with enthusiasm for the "in" music, entertainment, and activities. The offspring member might be a professional on a track to becoming like the parent-company member, but less wealthy and established and not yet able to go first class.

MARY SHELMAN *is the chairman of the board of RiceTec, based in Alvin, Texas. She is pursuing her doctorate in a joint program of Harvard University's Graduate School of Arts and Sciences and the Harvard Business School. Her research focuses on the future of brands.*

When any company considers taking its brand name into a new market (something each of Gordon's proposed changes would do), its senior managers should first weigh the benefits that the existing name would bring to the new market against the costs of using the name. That is standard, solid brand-management practice, but Gordon seems inclined to brush past it in his haste to get something under way. Slow down, Gordon. Where's the fire?

At first glance, the benefits of using the Transition name seem pretty clear: the existing equity in the brand could be leveraged through a new product; the brand could act as an assurance of quality and give consumers some basic information about the product's heritage and promise. But Gordon must ask himself certain questions. What is the message the existing brand brings to the new target market? Along with the positives, are there conflicts that may arise? That is, will too many potential customers automatically think they can't afford a club that bears the ultrapremium Transition name? In addition, how many people actually know about Transition? If the market is as select as it seems to be, would the name have any effect in the new, broader arena?

If Gordon determines that there is a benefit to using the Transition name, he must weigh it against two potential risks.

- **Cannibalization.** What happens if Gordon's current membership switches to his own lower-cost alternative? That seems unlikely, as the bundle of services available at the Ambassador clubs probably won't be the same as those offered at Printemps or at Transition's stand-alone locations, but Gordon should give it some thought. More likely is the danger that moving downmarket will put pressure on Gordon's current pricing structure: if he's having a hard time maintaining margins at this price level, how will he offer comparable services at lower cost?

- **Dilution of Equity in the Existing Brand Name.** As Kim pointed out, Transition is a Tiffany-type product: it is meant to be enjoyed by the privileged few. A large-scale expansion into a broader market will inevitably take Transition out of the exclusive arena. Gordon should think of exclusivity as a product attribute; how important is it to current customers? But exclusivity may mean different things to Transition's different members. For jet-setters, exclusivity may relate to the club's ego-intensive image. For business travelers, exclusivity might mean convenience: not having to wait and not having to share. If a current member uses facilities bearing the Transition name at an Ambassador hotel and finds herself waiting to use equipment, she may adjust the inherent value she places on the brand. Gordon might consider conducting a member survey to learn more. Transition's current users will probably be very forthcoming about what they value.

Brand name aside, Gordon should also ponder the organizational impact of his proposed actions. The skills needed to provide a luxury service are unlikely to be the same as those needed to manage a mass-market fitness chain, and Gordon has no first-mover advantage in the broader market. Right now, his company knows how to spend money better than it knows how to manage costs. And he'll need a completely new marketing and recruitment strategy: mass-market health clubs have tremendous membership turnover.

What if Gordon's team does turn its attention to the mass-market venture and successfully develops a new kind of club? Who will mind the store? If Gordon's star employees are learning a new set of skills and putting out fires in a new kind of business, the core business may suffer through neglect. In an organization in which excellent service is the business, that could be disastrous. That kind of a stretch could also have adverse affects on employee morale: a large staff will have dynamics that differ from those of a small, select team. Do Gordon's employees want to work for a different kind of company?

The changes Gordon proposes are not as simple as a new product offering: they signal a change in the company's core strategy. Ultimately, tailoring the pricing, partnering with another company, and even opening satellite corporate locations could be good ideas, as long as Gordon is clear about his objectives before he makes a move.

If he determines that expansion is the answer, he might consider these options: Why not partner with Clarkhouse? Or develop a separate, complementary chain called Transition II, which would specifically target younger business executives and travelers? An aging membership at the original Transition clubs probably means a high retention rate; Gordon can use that strength to great advantage if he tailors the core facilities to his current customers' changing needs and preps a new generation of members to join them.

Originally published in March–April 1995
Reprint 95205

Harvard Business Review *cases present common managerial dilemmas and offer concrete solutions from experts. As written, they are hypothetical, and the names used are fictitious.*

Should You Take Your Brand to Where the Action Is?

DAVID A. AAKER

Executive Summary

WHEN MARKETS TURN HOSTILE, it's no surprise that managers are tempted to extend their brands vertically—that is, to take their brands into a seemingly attractive market above or below their positions. And for companies chasing growth, the urge to move into booming premium or value segments also can be hard to resist. The draw is indeed strong; and in some instances, a vertical move is not merely justified but actually essential to survival—even for top brands, which have the advantages of economies of scale, brand equity, and retail clout. But beware: leveraging a brand to access upscale or downscale markets is more dangerous than it first appears.

Before making a move, then, managers should ascertain whether the rewards will be worth the risks. In general, David Aaker recommends that managers avoid vertical extensions whenever possible. There is an inherent contradiction in the very concept because brand equity is built in large part on image and perceived worth, and a vertical move can easily distort those qualities. Still, certain situations demand vertical extensions, and Aaker examines both the winners and the losers in the game. Managers may find themselves facing a situation that presents both an emerging opportunity and a strategic threat, and alternatives to vertical extensions may have even higher risks and costs. Furthermore, a number of brands have been extended vertically with complete success.

In after assessing the risks and rewards you conclude that a vertical extension is on the horizon, proceed with caution. And keep in mind that your challenge will be to leverage and protect the original brand while taking advantage of the new opportunity.

Wֶ HEN MARKETS TURN HOSTILE, it's no surprise that managers are tempted to extend their brands vertically—that is, to take brands into a seemingly attractive market above or below their current positions. And for companies chasing growth, the urge to move into booming premium or value segments also can be hard to resist. The draw is indeed strong; and in some instances, a vertical move is not merely justified but is actually essential to survival—even for top brands, which have the advantages of economies of scale, brand equity, and retail clout. But leveraging a brand to access upscale or downscale markets is more dangerous than it first appears. In fact, the battlefield is littered with dead and wounded brands that should serve as a warning to managers who are thinking about such extensions.

Before making a move, then, managers should ascertain whether the rewards will be worth the risks. How great is the opportunity? Should the brand retain its current position in a new market, or would it be better to reposition the brand entirely? What are the possible repercussions of such actions? Is a vertical extension the only choice? Would launching a new brand be a better alternative? The experiences of past winners and losers in the game can help managers answer those questions.

The challenge of vertical extensions is to leverage and protect the original brand while taking advantage of the new opportunity.

In general, I would recommend that managers avoid vertical extensions whenever possible. There is an inherent contradiction in the very concept because brand equity is built in large part on image and perceived worth, and a vertical move can easily distort those qualities. But *never* is a strong word. Managers may find themselves facing a situation that presents both an emerging opportunity and a strategic threat, and alternatives to vertical extensions may have even higher risks and costs. Furthermore, a number of brands have extended vertically with complete success. If after assessing the risks and rewards you conclude that a vertical extension is on the horizon, proceed with caution. And keep in mind that your challenge will be to leverage and protect the value of the original brand while taking advantage of the new opportunity.

Accessing Downscale Markets

Let's first consider taking a brand into value territory. Sometimes an opportunity emerges within a brand's current distribution channel—a boom in the value segment of any given product category sold through a supermarket, for example. More often, the opportunity is created or accompanied by its own low-cost distribution channel, and companies must prepare to sell their products through that channel. Specialty superstores such as Home Depot and Circuit City, for example, have created category-dominant outlets with price-sensitive customers and significant economies of scale. Warehouse clubs such as Price Club and discount stores such as Wal-Mart also are prime examples. And direct marketing, which has changed the cost structure in the computer industry and elsewhere, provides access to a value-oriented segment as well.

Who wouldn't be tempted to shift or at least to branch into a sizable and growing value market? This type of vertical extension promises increased volume and economies of scale. In addition, it promises protection from private-label and price-brand competitors, and from lower-quality, offshore entries. What's more, brands shift downward easily—sometimes inadvertently. The danger in a move down market is that once a brand has associated its name with a downscale offering—even if the move represents only a slight change in price or performance—it runs the risk of losing its stature as a higher-priced (and by inference, higher-quality) brand.

Consider the results of a research study conducted by Carol Motley, a professor at the University of Illinois at Champaign-Urbana, and Srinivas Reddy, a professor at the University of Georgia. When Motley and Reddy pre-

sented consumers with repositioning statements for
Kmart, a discount department store, and for Saks Fifth
Avenue, a high-end department store, they found that
people's attitudes toward Kmart did not change even
when the store was described as being upscale. In contrast, people reported that they thought less of Saks
when the store was described as being downscale or
even mainstream. Indeed, the damage that the Cadillac
Cimarron, the Cadillac version of a Chevrolet compact
car, caused the Cadillac brand in the 1980s attests to the
potential dangers of a downscale move.

One way to avoid any negative repercussions of
accessing a downscale market is to launch a new brand.
In 1993, the clothing retailer Gap found that competitors
were targeting its value-conscious customers by offering
Gap-like fashions for 20% to 30% below the company's
prices. So managers decided to test Gap Warehouse, a
store with merchandise offering the Gap flair but at a
cut below Gap quality and price. After a year, however,
managers found that the Gap connection was confusing
customers and cannibalizing the core brand's image. In
response, they renamed the new stores Old Navy Clothing Company—a brand that has become enormously
successful in its own right.

New brands, however, are not easy to introduce. First,
creating a new brand—building awareness, establishing
perceptions of identity and quality, and developing a
customer base—is expensive, often prohibitively so.
Even IBM, with its considerable resources, failed in its
effort to establish the Ambra, a relatively inexpensive
personal computer that was sourced in Asia and marketed between 1992 and 1994 by mail order in Europe
and the United States. Competing on price with Dell,
Gateway, and other IBM models, the Ambra could not

maintain a price that was low enough to compensate for its lack of brand equity. Second, new brands face distribution barriers. Retailers need to be convinced that a not-yet-established value brand can survive and add value to the retailer's line. They may refuse to carry a new product that does not offer the equity of an established brand.

REPOSITIONING THE ENTIRE BRAND

If launching a new brand is not an option, managers need to consider ways to leverage the power of their existing brand. There are several possibilities. One is to reposition the entire brand in a new market. The most direct way to do so is by dropping the brand's price—a move that can be called the *Marlboro option* in memory of that brand's stock-market-shaking 40-cent price cut on April 2, 1993. Indeed, Taco Bell, Post Cereals, AT&T, Procter & Gamble's Pampers, Amazon Books, and many other brands have pursued the Marlboro option in an attempt to make themselves more competitive in the face of price-oriented rivals and powerful retailers.

Managers can reposition an entire brand in a new downscale market by dropping its price, but beware the risks of that move.

That approach, however, can be quite risky. First, price cuts have enormous financial implications. A 20% price reduction, for example, exceeds the total profitability of most brands and will put significant pressure even on those brands that have enjoyed excessive prices and margins. In addition, competitors—especially weaker ones—will have little choice but to match or exceed any permanent price decrease. Price wars are a very real threat.

Second, the Marlboro option can do substantial damage to a brand's image. A price reduction will likely make price the basis for competition and reinforce consumers' perceptions about a brand's lack of differentiation—particularly when it comes to quality. Taco Bell, in an aggressive attempt to improve volume and to capitalize on its cost advantage over other fast-food restaurants, introduced a "value" menu in 1990 that successfully boosted sales at the expense of other fast-food chains. In 1995, facing a downturn in sales, the company tried to take that strategy one step further by introducing an "extreme value" menu. That move has proved unsuccessful, so the company has decided to try to reverse its image and upgrade its menu with better-quality products at higher price tags. Customers, however, are resisting the move. Clearly, it will not be easy to turn what has become a solid value image into something more.

One way to reduce the risk of a tarnished brand image is to provide a rationale for the price move in a way that implies that quality has not been sacrificed. In 1992, Procter & Gamble launched an everyday-low-price program as part of its strategy to create more efficient product-delivery systems to retailers and consumers. For retailers, the program reduced incentives to engage in costly practices such as forward buying and diverting. For consumers, it made shopping much less complicated. Both retailers and consumers interpreted the move as being part of a larger coherent strategy.

Companies also can mitigate the risk of a damaged image by providing additional support for the brand while lowering its price. Marlboro engaged in aggressive advertising and launched the Marlboro Adventure Team promotion (investing $200 million in rewarding its loyal customers with outdoor adventure offerings) both before and after its price cut. Investing in a brand at a time when its profit margin is going to drop, as Marlboro did, is at first glance an unpalatable course. Understandably, most managers want to preserve as much of their brand's margin as possible. Without increased investment, however, the brand risks being recognized and sold on price alone.

Of course, if a brand has become so weak that revitalization is not feasible, there may be no brand equity to risk. Schlitz beer, attempting to cut costs in the mid-1970s, began to use cheaper ingredients and processes that resulted in a beer that tasted as good as the original but turned cloudy and lost fizz when left on the shelf for too long. The company recalled 10 million bottles and cans in 1976 and went back to its old methods of making beer. But its image—and its sales—never recovered. Schlitz became a price brand after its sales fell from greater than 17 million barrels in 1977 to fewer than 1 million barrels in the late 1980s. It had nothing to lose and no other feasible alternatives.

It is important to recognize that managing a brand on price is different than managing a brand on an image of quality or style. Managers of price brands should reduce brand support and create a cost advantage (or at least avoid a cost disadvantage) with respect to logistics, production, price, and service. It is fatal to try to compete as a price brand with a cost disadvantage.

The ultimate way for a brand to compete in a downscale market is to create value and differentiation so that the brand no longer seems overpriced. Procter &

Gamble has adopted this strategy successfully time and again. Tide's managers, for example, have made dozens of innovative improvements in the product and its packaging over the years to inhibit the tendency of the brand to drift toward commodity status.

USING SUB-BRANDS

If the bulk of a brand's customers are willing to pay a price premium, there is no benefit to moving the entire brand down market in order to attract new customers. Companies will merely be trading one set of customers for another. In that case, managers should instead consider a *sub-brand:* a brand with its own name that uses the name of its parent brand in some capacity to bolster equity, such as Courtyard by Marriott or Gillette Good News razors. In the case of downscale offerings, the role of sub-brands is to help managers differentiate new offerings from parent brands while using the parent's equity to influence consumers. The idea is both to maintain the parent's credibility and prestige regardless of how the sub-brand performs and to protect the original brand from cannibalization. (In most cases, the question is not whether the parent brand will be adversely affected by the downscale sub-brand but how to keep that negative impact to a minimum.)

There are three types of relationships between parent brands and sub-brands. First, the parent brand can act as an *endorser* of the sub-brand. In this case, the sub-brand is the more dominant of the two and drives consumers' decisions to buy a product or service as well as their perceptions of the experience using the product or service. Second, the parent and sub-brand can be *co-drivers* with roughly equal influence on consumers. Third, the parent can retain its primary influence as a *driver,* and the sub-brand can act as a *descriptor*—a word or phrase that tells consumers that the company is offering a slight variation on the same product or service they have come to know. Keep in mind that there are grades of each type of relationship. An endorser can range from a tiny logo in the corner of a product's package to a more prominent endorsement that falls short of co-driver status. Some co-driver sub-brands have more modest driver roles than others. And some descriptor brands play limited driver roles.

When consumers buy a car such as the Ford Taurus, are they purchasing a Ford, a Taurus, or a combination of the two?

Put simply, sub-brands vary in the extent to which they influence consumers' purchase decisions and their experience using the product or service. Do consumers buy and use a Ford, a Taurus, or a combination of the two? When they purchase a Ford Taurus, are they expecting a certain style and level of performance from Ford or from Taurus? What do they expect when they decide to buy a Ford? What do they expect when they decide to buy a Taurus?

Let's examine in greater depth the three ways a parent brand can relate to its sub-brand.

Endorsers. John Deere's foray into value lawn tractors provides a good illustration of an endorser relationship. John Deere was well known for making a lawn tractor that sold for approximately $2,000 through full-service specialty dealers. Although the manufacturer was still able to command that price in the specialty market, volume retailers such as Sears and Home Depot had begun to serve a growing portion (around 30%) of that market, selling products at half John Deere's prices. So the company introduced an endorsed sub-brand for the value retailers: a low-cost tractor, Sabre from John Deere, that featured an inexpensive design and a different color and feel than John Deere's other products.

Similarly, when Marriott International wanted to enter the business-traveler and economy-family markets, it introduced Courtyard by Marriott and Fairfield Inn by Marriott—two chains that were clearly very different in location, ambiance, and service both from each other and from the parent brand. The Marriott endorsement gives consumers the assurance that these value entries will deliver on their promises to customers just as Marriott does.

Consider also the Hobart Company, which makes an industrial-grade mixer for use in bakeries and restaurants. Managers decided to create an inexpensive mixer for use in commercial and industrial kitchens to compete with offshore entries without damaging its flagship "gold standard" Hobart mixer line. In 1996, the company introduced Medalist from the Hobart Company. Medalist mixers were lighter than Hobart mixers. In addition, they were made with less costly materials and construction processes; and they had a color and logo distinct from those of the flagship Hobart.

Sub-brands vary in the extent to which they influence consumers' purchase decisions and their experience using the offering.

When a company offers an endorsed sub-brand, there are three brands at work. The parent brand itself is split into two: a product brand and an organizational brand.

The product brand remains as it was, a premium brand delivering a certain image and associated benefits. By contrast, the Hobart Company has become an organizational brand that endorses the sub-brand, Medalist. Medalist itself is a new product brand. Thus the parent brand, Hobart, is separated from the sub-brand, Medalist, by the organizational brand, the Hobart Company.

The endorser strategy provides an excellent chance to minimize damage and reduce the threat of cannibalization to the parent brand. Keep in mind that all three brands need to be managed actively. Managers of the Hobart Company brand name, for example, would concentrate their efforts on intangible attributes, such as being innovative or having a customer-oriented culture. Managers of the Hobart product brand would continue to manage that brand as they had. Managers of the Medalist sub-brand would focus on promoting specific qualities such as the brand's functional benefits or its distinct personality.

Co-drivers. Gillette Good News illustrates a successful co-driver relationship. Gillette Good News disposable razors are a definite cut below "the best a man can get" that is the Gillette legacy in shaving. But disposable razors are qualitatively different from the upscale razors such as Sensor and Atra with which Gillette has long held a technological edge. Gillette could provide a rationale for a disposable brand by being the best in the disposable category. But the Good News user's personality—younger and more carefree than the traditionally masculine and sophisticated Gillette persona—plays a key role in distinguishing the disposable brand from the rest of the line. Both brand names—Gillette and Good News—influence the customer's decision to buy the product.

United Airlines' United Express brand is another good example. The United Airlines brand provides United Express, a commuter line, with the convenience of connections to United flights and a reputation for safety. There is no cannibalization because the flights do not compete. United Express is differentiated from its parent brand by its lower level of on-board service, its use of smaller planes, and its less formal (even funky) personality.

Co-driver relationships are not always so successful. Consider Kodak Funtime film. Kodak introduced Funtime in 1994 to combat price brands and private-label film. But less than two years after its launch, managers took Funtime off the market. The reason? It is likely that many Funtime customers already were Kodak customers and were attracted to Funtime because it was a Kodak film at a lower price. Because that price was still significantly higher than that of the value brands on the market, Kodak Funtime was not that attractive to price-oriented customers. The reality was that the value brands were always going to maintain a price gap unless Kodak engaged in a real price war. It also seemed likely that Funtime was creating confusion among Kodak's loyal customers and was hurting the core brand's image.

Drivers. Of the three types of relationships, a driver parent brand with a descriptor sub-brand is the most risky. The parent brand is vulnerable to cannibalization because very little distinguishes one brand from the other. The risk of cannibalization is greatest when a descriptor (such as ValuePoint or Thrifty) signifies merely a lower-quality offering. The risk is minimized when the descriptor signals a different application (such as Masterlock's Lockers and Bikes line of lighter locks, which are designed for a completely different use than Masterlock's Sheds and Gates line of locks) or a slightly different target market (such as Fender Starter, an electric guitar designed for youngsters just beginning to learn the instrument, which is offered by a company whose other brands are marketed toward professional, experienced musicians).

Mercedes provides a good illustration of a driver brand that has successfully accessed a downscale market with a descriptor sub-brand. In the early 1980s, Mercedes introduced what is now its C Class, a small car to compete with the BMW 3 series, as well as with Acura and Lexus. Now priced around $30,000, the line sells nearly 30,000 cars annually in the United States (around one-third of all Mercedes sales in the United States). How could a brand that has historically been identified with prestige and that offers a car selling for more than $100,000 pull off this kind of downscale move? First, Mercedes delivered a quality product. Second, the C Class introduction was accompanied by an intensive effort to reposition the core brand's message from prestige to performance. Third, marketing for the C Class aggressively targeted young buyers. The C Class name creates a distinction that allows the sub-brand to attract a slightly different consumer, but it does not drive that consumer's decision to buy the car. The Mercedes brand name retains that power.

Consider, too, Filene's Basement. Since 1908, Filene's department store has sold off-price goods (that is, goods that need to be marked down and sold) in its basement. Displays were rather crude, and many shoppers enjoyed the pushing and shoving and absence of changing rooms that were a part of the scene. Filene's Basement, very different from the upscale main floors, actually became a strong enough brand to become a minichain, which performed well but ultimately became a casualty of an ill-advised leveraged buyout in the late 1980s.

Accessing Upscale Markets

The motivation for moving a brand from a mainstream market into an upscale arena is clear: high-end markets enjoy much higher margins than middle markets do. What's more, emerging high-end segments often seem to revitalize entire groups of tired products. Consider what microbreweries, designer coffees, luxury cars, and even upscale water have done for their respective categories. Newly popular, newly exciting markets—and their margins—beckon, but can a brand that is firmly established in a mainstream market alter its image enough to compete?

The issue is one of credibility. Most consumers will question whether a formerly inexpensive brand will have the knowledge, capability, and will to operate an upscale brand and deliver the expected functional and emotional benefits. Even brands that enjoy solid reputations are suspect. For example, the Holiday Inn brand name, which stood for comfortable, unpretentious family hotels, was a real handicap when it was used on Holiday Inn's Crowne Plaza hotels, which targeted an upscale market. Eventually, and not surprisingly, the parent company dropped the Holiday Inn connection and let Crowne Plaza compete on its own. The cases of downscale brands with lower-quality images evolving into higher-quality, more upscale brands are very rare. Toyota represents such a case, but changing its image took more than a decade, involved impressive product improvements, and cost billions of dollars in advertising.

As in downscale moves, one way to access a high-end market is to launch or acquire a new brand. For instance, because Honda managers believed that the Honda name would be a fatal barrier to the company's ability to succeed in an upscale market dominated by BMW and Mercedes, they developed the Acura brand. Toyota and Nissan followed suit with the Lexus and Infiniti brands. Similarly, Black & Decker used a new brand, DeWalt, when it created a line of tools for construction professionals in 1992. The company's research showed that construction professionals associated Black & Decker with the do-it-yourself market segment, dustbusters, and even popcorn poppers. The company realized that such associations did not bode well for a premium line of tools.

The fact that Toyota owns Lexus or that Black & Decker owns DeWalt need not be a secret. In fact, having a "shadow" endorsement can help reduce consumers' suspicions that the new brand will not have staying power. By not overtly associating its name with Toyota, Lexus says to consumers that it has an individual identity—and that statement is more important than whether consumers learn of the connection.

Again, however, creating a new brand can be extremely expensive—especially if competitors include well-established brands. Toyota, for instance, made a tremendous investment in Lexus to help it become a player. Sometimes it is possible to reduce the cost by licensing an upscale brand name from another product class—say, a clothing line using the Tiffany name or a line of furniture using Mercedes—but that approach forgoes the strategic power of owning the upscale brand.

REPOSITIONING THE ENTIRE BRAND

The story here is brief. Straightforward repositioning from a mainstream or value market into an upscale one is nearly impossible. A mainstream brand simply lacks the upscale associations—such as user image, brand personality, and perceived quality—that are necessary to convince customers that the product or service should command a premium price. What's more, an upscale move, even if successful, can risk sacrificing the parent brand's existing customer base—its major asset. Current customers may become uncomfortable with the brand as it transforms in order to attract a new market. Sears Roebuck & Company is one of the few companies that has had some success in this area. With exceptional advertising and an enormous investment in changing its stores' environments, Sears has moved a bit upscale, particularly in women's clothing. But in so doing, the company has walked a fine line: its loyal, value-oriented customers have specific expectations about what they are getting for their money, and they may be wondering if the new brand image will change that equation.

USING SUB-BRANDS

Sub-brands play the same role in upscale moves as they do in downscale ventures: they help managers differentiate their new premium offerings from the original brands while using the equity of those parent brands to influence consumers' purchase decisions.

Sub-brands used in up-market moves also vary with respect to the distance they create between the new entry and the parent brand. When the parent is an endorser, as with Uncle Ben's Country Inn rice, the

brands are relatively separate—with the sub-brand
establishing its own identity and influencing consumers'
purchase decisions. When the parent and sub-brand are
co-drivers, as with MJB EuroRoast coffee or Black &
Decker Quantum tools,
the influence of each
brand on purchase deci-
sions is roughly equal.
When the parent brand
is a driver accompanied
by a sub-brand descrip-
tor, as with Trefethen
Library Reserve wines or GE Profile appliances, the sub-
brand does not develop a unique identity at all; rather, it
indicates an upscale variant of the parent brand.

*Managers contemplating a
move up market
might want to consider
positioning a sub-
brand at the low end of the
upscale arena.*

When contemplating an upscale sub-brand, it is critical to consider the new offering's potential customers. Is
the brand really going to attract people who habitually
purchase the highest-end goods? Or is the sub-brand's
greatest potential actually somewhere in between the
highest offerings and the parent brand's position? Sometimes it's best to position a sub-brand at the low end of
the upscale market. A "value" premium offering can be
attractive to consumers who consider themselves independent thinkers with no need to buy image in order to
impress people. Low-end premium brands also are
attractive to people who would like to be part of an
upscale niche but can't afford the higher-end offerings.
When managers of one major coffee brand decided to
enter the designer coffee market with a sub-brand, they
conducted extensive research on what they thought to
be their target market—yuppie consumers—and positioned the sub-brand accordingly. The product was successful, but subsequent research revealed that the yuppie market was not well represented among the

sub-brand's customers; the market instead turned out to be mainstream consumers who were trading up.

Keep in mind that the bigger the vertical leap, the tougher it is to make. Take Rice-A-Roni. Because the parent brand is strongly associated with everyday meals, its upscale sub-brand, Rice-A-Roni Savory Classics, did not work. Uncle Ben's, however, is positioned as a basic product that has a certain simple elegance. Because the original brand is flexible, a sub-brand like Uncle Ben's Country Inn Rice Alfredo Homestyle pilaf works as an upscale entry. The Uncle Ben's name, though not upscale itself, is not incompatible with the new offering or context.

The safest bet for an upscale sub-brand is a driver-descriptor strategy because it positions the new offering against the parent brand rather than against its new upscale competitors. *Special edition, premium, profes-sional, gold,* or *platinum* descriptors—especially when they are offered at a premium price—can be very effective. They send the message that the upscale entry is like the parent brand but tangibly better. Wineries use *private reserve, library reserve,* or *limited edition* to capture the higher end of a market. Similarly, airlines have *connoisseur class.* (See "Strategies for Sub-brands: Minimizing Risk" at the end of this article for some general guidelines on using sub-brands in upscale and down-scale moves.)

How Much Can One Brand Handle?

In rare cases, a single brand can stretch successfully from value to mainstream to premium markets. Sony is such a brand. For years, the Sony brand has freely spanned quality levels in several product classes. For example, the Sony Walkman ranges in price from $25 to more than $500 without confusing customers or damaging the brand. The wisdom of Sony's strategy is nevertheless debatable. It can certainly be argued that what Sony has gained in brand visibility and leverage compensates for any negative repercussions from its downscale offerings. But we can never know how much better off Sony might have been had it protected its brand name and created a separate value brand for the lower end of the markets. It is also worth noting that even Sony has not taken its name to all its brands across the board. When Sony purchased the Loews movie theater chain, it initially put its name on the theaters. Realizing that most of the Loews theaters were old and did not deliver a movie experience that was compatible with the Sony name, the company soon withdrew the association and placed the Loews name back on most of the theaters— with the exception of a few newer ones that featured IMAX sound and reinforced much of what the Sony brand represented.

Sony's experience is indeed uncommon. It may be possible to have two separate positions—a premium position for the mainstream market and a value position for the value market—if the two markets are very separate with respect to communication and distribution. The markets, however, are rarely that distinct.

Consider Levi Strauss and CitiBank. Both are high-end, prestigious brands in the Far East and Europe but are mainstream, functional brands in the United States. The brands' similar problems with conflicting images have been mitigated in part by the geographical distance among their markets; but even with such a buffer, the companies face difficulties. CitiBank sends mixed messages to its global customers who do business with the company in several countries—a growing market segment that is becoming increasingly important to please.

And because the retail price for its products sold in the United States is often far below the wholesale price in Europe, Levi Strauss is plagued by so-called gray sales—that is, goods being sold through unauthorized but legal channels. For example, Tesco, a leading retail chain of stores in the United Kingdom, recently bought 45,000 men's 501 jeans on the gray market and sold them for far less than the prices charged in stores supplied directly by Levi Strauss. The result? Authorized retailers lose the motivation to recommend or carry the line, and customers lose the emotional benefits associated with buying authentic Levi's at full price.

Keep these cases in mind when you are considering a vertical extension. Evaluate and reevaluate the opportunities and the risks. Study your brand's position, its strengths, its weaknesses, its message. If you are contemplating an upscale or a downscale move, strongly consider launching a new brand. If you have the luxury of controlling a portfolio of brands, think about using them to rationalize the line as General Electric did in appliances by using RCA as a price brand and Hotpoint as a value brand, and by reserving GE, GE Profile, and GE Monogram for the upscale offerings. If you can purchase a new brand, do so. Reposition at your own risk, and use sub-brands only if you can take the same care with their launches as you do with your core brand.

Strategies for Sub-brands: Minimizing Risk

When Moving Down Market . . .

- Try to create a qualitatively different offering aimed at a distinct segment. Position the entry as the best of a distinct new product or service offering. For instance, Medalist by the Hobart Company, Courtyard by Marriott, and Sabre from John Deere sharply differ in look and feel from their respective parent brands. And Gillette Good News, Courtyard by Marriott, and the Mercedes C Class are physically different from Gillette Sensor, Marriott Marquis, and the Mercedes S Class. Furthermore, these value offerings target distinct segments and aspire to be the best in their respective segments. Differentiating a value offering from its parent brand works best when physical differences are clearly apparent. It is more difficult to create a distinct image with such products as film or fertilizer.

- **Think about elevating the parent brand when the value entry is launched.** It is easier to create the necessary distance between the parent brand and the sub-brand if the parent is moved slightly upscale. For example, if instead of merely introducing a value sub-brand of a line of tools you upgraded the original line and gave it a sub-brand name like ProChoice at the same time you introduced a value name like ThriftMaster, you would increase the separation between the brands and reduce the risk of cannibalization. In this manner, Gillette's innovative premium sub-brands such as Atra and Sensor enhanced the distinction between Gillette Good News and the Gillette brand.

- **Be cautious about price premiums.** When the core brand is well known, it is tempting to try to command higher prices—even in value markets. But people who shop for value are sensitive to price, regardless of brand name. Don't count on your brand's equity in the new arena. Mercedes managers understand that the C Class cars are priced competitively, and that's one reason for their success. In contrast, Kodak's Funtime film suffered because Kodak managers launched it as a value brand yet priced it well above the target competition. Similarly,

Armani Exchange—an attempt to offer the Armani name in a casual-clothing competitor of the Gap and the Limited— failed after some initial sales success in part because customers eventually balked at the price difference. (Armani Exchange T-shirts, for example, were two-and-a-half times more expensive than competitors' offerings.)

- **Consider a parent-child metaphor.** A parent-child metaphor suggests a distinction between personalities and can help provide cohesion and logic to a brand strategy that, because it spans several markets, involves some very basic inconsistencies. The value entry subbrand can be a son or daughter of the parent brand. This son or daughter would have the same "genes" as the parent but may not yet have matured into a top-of-the-line product or service. In addition to being geared toward a younger and less affluent market, the son or daughter subbrand can be expected to have a distinct personality. The nature of this personality will depend on the product setting, the user profile, and the parent brand. A son or daughter with youth and vigor might be appropriate for a motorcycle, bicycle, or health club. A serious son might reassure consumers of the reliability of a new line of lawn equipment or trucks. And a spontaneous and fun-loving daughter might be the right image for a line of women's clothes.

When Moving Up Market . . .

- **Make the vertical leap reasonable.** How far up market should a brand move? Sub-brands accessing premium markets often do better when they are positioned at the low end of the segment. The claim that a product is superior to a company's mainstream brand is less of a stretch than the claim that it is superior—or even equal—to established premium brands.

- **Differentiate the upscale entry.** Regardless of the distance between the mainstream and the upscale market, it is important to give the new offering distinct characteristics. Black & Decker's Quantum line of equipment, developed for the 20 million or more serious do-it-yourself consumers in the United States, is a good example of a sub-brand that is clearly distinct both from its core brand and from DeWalt, its line for construction professionals. The Quantum line offers several products that are distinct from other Black & Decker offerings, among them a "dustless" drill that uses a specially designed vacuum system. That product and others—as well as such Quantum-specific services as the *Shop Talk* newsletter and the Power-Source telephone advice program—give the new line credibility and help position it well above the core brand's line of tools. Upscale sub-brands also can benefit from distinctive looks. Quantum tools are silver with yellow print, in sharp contrast to the metallic green of the core Black & Decker line. All cues—advertising, packaging, name, look, and feel—contribute to the sub-brand's distinct personality and thus help it establish itself.

- **Redefine success by assigning the upscale sub-brand a "silver bullet" role.** In other words, use the sub-brand as a tool to revitalize the core brand. Gallo did just that with its Ernest and Julio Gallo Varietals, an upscale sub-brand of a solid value brand. Gallo's biggest sales came from its trademark jug wine, which had begun to face stiff competition from slightly more upscale brands such as Glen Ellen. To protect itself, the enormous Gallo enterprise needed to move up a small notch—a daunting task. So it introduced the Ernest and Julio Gallo Varietals: a new line of wines offered at prices more than double those of its jug wine, with labels, bottle types, and advertising to befit an upscale entry. The sub-brand's target market was not high-end consumers but rather the core Gallo consumer. The company knew that many current Gallo customers would never purchase an Ernest and Julio Gallo Varietal, but the high-end product gave Gallo the opportunity to influence them in a different way. The company used the sub-brand's associations of quality to elevate perceptions of the entire Gallo brand.

Originally published in September–October 1997
Reprint 97501

Extend Profits, Not Product Lines

JOHN A. QUELCH AND DAVID KENNY

Executive Summary

IN THE LAST TEN YEARS, products have proliferated in every category of consumer goods and services, and the deluge shows few signs of letting up. Most companies are pursuing product expansion strategies—in particular, line extensions—full steam ahead. But more and more evidence is indicating the pitfalls of such aggressive tactics.

John Quelch and David Kenny explain that companies have pursued line extensions as part of their marketing strategies for several reasons: Managers perceive extensions as a low-cost, low-risk way to meet the needs of various customer segments; line extensions can satisfy consumers' desires by providing a wide variety of goods under a single brand; and managers often use extensions as a short-term competitive device to increase a brand's control over limited shelf space.

But the strategic role of each item becomes muddled when a line is oversegmented. Furthermore, a company that extends its line risks undermining brand loyalty. Line extensions rarely expand category demand, and retailers can't provide more shelf space to a category just because there are more products. Most important, the costs of line-extension proliferation can remain hidden.

Some companies, such as Procter & Gamble, Chrysler, and a leading U.S. snack foods company, have discovered that a carefully focused and well-managed line can increase profits and sales volume. Quelch and Kenny describe how marketing managers can sharpen their product-line strategies by improving cost accounting, allocating resources to popular products, researching consumer behavior, coordinating marketing efforts, working with channel partners, and fostering a climate in which product-line deletions are not only accepted but also encouraged.

IN THE LAST TEN YEARS, products have proliferated at an unprecedented rate in every category of consumer goods and services, and the deluge shows few signs of letting up. Most companies are pursuing product expansion strategies—in particular, line extensions—full steam ahead. At the same time, however, more and more evidence is indicating the pitfalls of such aggressive expansion if it is not well managed: hidden cost increases, weakened brand images, and troubled relations with distributors and retailers.

Unfortunately, in most organizations, managers have no incentive to question their product-line-extension strategies. Marketers argue for more line extensions to serve an increasingly segmented marketplace, and sales managers use extensions to justify hiring more salespeople. While manufacturing managers are concerned about the complexity of production and the finance department has a clear interest in cost control, the information systems needed to cull the data that would justify a more focused product line are often not in place.

How can companies encourage an objective assessment of product-line strategy? Ultimately, the remedy lies in proving that a focused, well-managed line leads to greater profits and is an asset for the entire organization. But first, senior managers must overcome some ingrained beliefs about the advantages of line extensions.

The Lure of Line Extensions

Seven factors explain why so many companies have pursued line extensions as a significant part of their marketing strategies.

Customer segmentation. Managers perceive line extensions as a low-cost, low-risk way to meet the needs of various customer segments, and by using more sophisticated and lower-cost market research and direct-marketing techniques, they can identify and target finer segments more effectively than ever before. In addition, the depth of audience-profile information for television, radio, and print media has improved; managers can now translate complex segmentation schemes into efficient advertising plans.

Consumer desires. More consumers than ever are switching brands and trying products they've never used before. Line extensions try to satisfy the desire for "something different" by providing a wide variety of goods under a single brand umbrella. Such extensions, companies hope, fulfill customers' desires while keeping them loyal to the brand franchise.

Moreover, according to studies conducted by the Point-of-Purchase Advertising Institute, consumers now make around two-thirds of their purchase decisions about grocery and health-and-beauty products on impulse while they are in the store. Line extensions, if stocked by the retailer, can help a brand increase its share of shelf space, thus attracting consumer attention. When marketers coordinate the packaging and labeling across all items in a brand line, they can achieve an attention-getting billboard effect on the store shelf or display stand and thus leverage the brand's equity.

Pricing breadth. Managers often tout the superior quality of extensions and set higher prices for these offerings than for core items. In markets subject to slow volume growth, marketers can then increase unit profitability by trading current customers up to these "premium" products. In this way, even cannibalized sales are profitable—at least in the short run.

In a similar spirit, some line extensions are priced lower than the lead product. For example, American Express offers the Optima card for a lower annual fee than its standard card, and Marriott introduced the hotel chain Courtyard by Marriott to provide a lower-priced alternative to its standard hotels. Extensions give marketers the opportunity to offer a broader range of price points in order to capture a wider audience.

Excess capacity. In the 1980s, many manufacturing operations added faster production lines to improve efficiency and quality. The same organizations, however, did not necessarily retire existing production lines. The resulting excess capacity encourages the introduction of line extensions that require only minor adaptations of current products.

Short-term gain. Next to sales promotions, line extensions represent the most effective and least imaginative way to increase sales quickly and inexpensively. The development time and costs of line extensions are far more predictable than they are for new brands, and less cross-functional integration is required.

In fact, few brand managers are willing to invest the time or assume the career risk to shepherd new brands to market. They are well aware of the following: major brands have staying power (almost all of the 20 brands that lead in consumer awareness were on that list 20 years ago); the cost of a successful brand launch in the United States is now estimated at $30 million, versus $5 million for a line extension; new branded products have a poor success rate (only one in five commercialized new products lasts longer than one year on the market); and consumer goods technologies have matured and are widely accessible. Line extensions offer quick rewards with minimal risk.

Most managers will extend a line before they will invest the time or assume the career risk to launch a new brand.

Finally, senior managers often set objectives for the percentages of future sales to come from products recently introduced. At the same time, under pressure from Wall Street for quarterly earnings increases, they do not invest enough in the long-term research and development needed to create genuinely new products. Such actions necessarily encourage line extensions.

Competitive intensity. Mindful of the link between market share and profitability, managers often see extensions as a short-term competitive device that increases a brand's control over limited retail shelf space and, if overall demand for the category can be expanded, also increases the space available to the entire category. Frequent line extensions are often used by major brands to raise the admission price to the category for new branded or private-label competitors and to drain the limited resources of third- and fourth-place brands. Crest and Colgate toothpastes, for example, both available in more than 35 types and package sizes, have increased their market shares in the last decade at the expense of smaller brands that have not been able to keep pace with their new offerings.

Trade pressure. The proliferation of different retail channels for consumer products, from club stores to hypermarkets, pressures manufacturers to offer broad and varied product lines. While retailers object to the proliferation of marginally differentiated and "me-too" line extensions, trade accounts themselves contribute to stock-keeping unit (SKU) proliferation by demanding either special package sizes to fit their particular marketing strategies (for example, bulk packages or multi-packs for low-price club stores) or customized, derivative models that impede comparison shopping by consumers. Black & Decker, for example, offers 19 types of irons, in part to enable competing retailers to stock different items from the line.

The Pitfalls of Proliferation

Against this backdrop, it's easy to see why so many managers have been swept into line-extension mania. But, as more managers are discovering, the problems and risks associated with extension proliferation are formidable.

Weaker line logic. Managers often extend a line without removing any existing items. As a result, the line may expand to the point of oversegmentation, and the strategic role of each item becomes muddled. Salespeople should be able to explain the commercial logic for each item. If they cannot, retailers turn to their own data—the information collected by checkout scanners—to help them decide which items to stock. Invariably, fewer retailers stock an entire line. As a result, manufacturers lose control of the presentation of their lines at the point of sale, and the chance that a consumer's preferred size or flavor will be out of stock increases.

What's more, a disorganized product line can confuse consumers, motivating those less interested in the category to seek out a simple, all-purpose product, such as All Temperature Cheer in the laundry detergent category.

Lower brand loyalty. Some marketers mistakenly believe that loyalty is an attitude instead of understanding that loyalty is the behavior of purchasing the same product repeatedly. In the past 50 years, many of the oldest and strongest brands have had two and three generations of customers buying and using products in the same way.

People do not eat more, drink more, or wash their hair more just because they have more products from which to choose.

When a company extends its line, it risks disrupting the patterns and habits that underlie brand loyalty and reopening the entire purchase decision.

Although line extensions can help a single brand satisfy a consumer's diverse needs, they can also motivate
customers to seek variety and, hence, indirectly encourage brand switching. In the short run, line extensions
may increase the market share of the overall brand franchise. But if cannibalization and a shift in marketing
support decrease the share held by the lead product, the
long-term health of the franchise will be weakened. This
is particularly true when line extensions diffuse rather
than reinforce a brand's image in the eyes of long-
standing consumers without attracting new customers.

Underexploited ideas. By bringing important new
products to market as line extensions, many companies
leave money on the table. Some product ideas are big
enough to warrant a new brand. The line extension serves
the career goals of a manager on an existing brand better
than a new brand does, but long-term profits are often
sacrificed in favor of short-term risk management.

Stagnant category demand. Line extensions rarely
expand total category demand. People do not eat or
drink more, wash their hair more, or brush their teeth
more frequently simply because they have more products from which to choose. In fact, a review of several
product categories shows no positive correlation
between category growth and line extensions. (See the
chart "Line Extensions Don't Increase Demand.") If anything, there is an inverse correlation as marketers try in
vain to reinvigorate declining categories and protect
their shelf space through insignificant line extensions.

Poorer trade relations. On average, the number of
consumer-packaged-goods SKUs grew 16% each year

from 1985 to 1992, while retail shelf space expanded by only 1.5% each year. Retailers cannot provide more shelf space to a category simply because there are more products within it. They have responded to the flood by rationing their shelf space, stocking slow-moving items only when promoted by their manufacturers, and charging manufacturers slotting fees to obtain shelf space for new items and failure fees for items that do not meet target sales within two or three months. As manufacturers' credibility has declined, retailers have allocated more shelf space to their own private-label products. Competition among manufacturers for the limited slots still available escalates

Line Extensions Don't Increase Demand

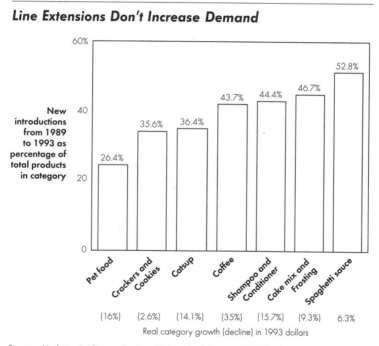

Sources: *Marketing Intelligence Services; Nielsen North America*, SCANTRACK

overall promotion expenditures and shifts margin to the increasingly powerful retailers.

More competitor opportunities. Share gains from line extensions are typically short-lived. New products can be matched quickly by competitors. What's more, line-extension proliferation reduces the retailer's average turnover rate and profit per SKU. This can expose market leaders to brands that do not attempt to match all the leaders' line extensions but instead offer product lines concentrated on the most popular line extensions. As a result, on a per-SKU basis, brands such as SmithKline Beecham's Aquafresh toothpaste can deliver a higher direct product profit to the retailer than brands with larger shares and more SKUs.

Increased costs. Companies expect and plan for a number of costs associated with a line extension, such as market research, product and packaging development, and the product launch. The brand group may also expect certain increases in administrative costs: planning the promotion calendar takes more time when an extension is added to the line, as does deciding on the advertising allocations between the core brand and its extensions. But managers may not foresee the following pitfalls:

- Fragmentation of the overall marketing effort and dilution of the brand image.

- Increased production complexity resulting from shorter production runs and more frequent line changeovers. (These are somewhat mitigated by the ability to customize products toward the end of an otherwise standardized production process with flexible manufacturing systems.)

- More errors in forecasting demand and increased logistics complexity, resulting in increased remnants and larger buffer inventories to avoid stockouts.

- Increased supplier costs due to rush orders and the inability to buy the most economic quantities of raw materials.

- Distraction of the research and development group from new product development.

The unit costs for multi-item lines can be 25% to 45% higher than the theoretical cost of producing only the most popular item in the line. (See the chart "The Cost of Variety.") The inability of most line extensions to increase demand in a category makes it hard for companies to recover the extra costs through increases in volume. And even if a line extension can command a higher

The Cost of Variety

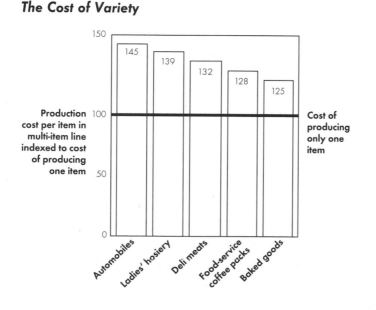

unit price, the expanded gross margin is usually insufficient to recover such dramatic incremental unit costs.

The costs of line-extension proliferation remain hidden for several reasons. First, traditional cost-accounting systems allocate overheads to items in proportion to their sales. These systems, which are common even among companies pursuing a low-cost-producer strategy, overburden the high sellers and undercharge the slow movers. A detailed cost-allocation study of one line found that only 15% of the items accounted for all the brand's profits. That means that 85% of the items in the line offered little or no return to justify their full costs.

Second, during the 1980s, marketers were able to raise prices to cushion the cost of line extensions. A review of 12 packaged-goods companies shows that price increases in excess of raw-material-cost increases contributed 10.4 additional percentage points to gross margins between 1980 and

Traditional accounting systems can hide the costs of line-extension proliferation.

1990, but 8.6 points were absorbed by increased selling, general, and administrative (SG&A) costs. Now that low inflation and the recent recession have restricted marketers' ability to raise prices, margins will be more clearly squeezed by new line extensions.

Third, line extensions are usually added one at a time. As a result, managers rarely consider the costs of complexity, even though adding several individual extensions may change the cost structure of the entire line.

Once a company's senior managers take the time to examine the downside of aggressive line extension, rationalizing the product line is a fairly straightforward process. Consider the case of a leading U.S. snack foods company, which we will call Snackco. For several years,

Snackco extended its line at a dizzying pace. More recently, the company has discovered that a carefully focused line increases both profits and sales.

Snackco's Fall and Rise

In the late 1980s, Snackco was active in leadership markets, that is, markets the company dominated, and competitive markets, in which Snackco was at parity or weaker than its main competitor. Over time, Snackco's product line had proliferated: between 1987 and 1989, the company had increased its new offerings by 20%. During that period, however, overall sales remained flat.

Alarmed by the data, Snackco's president and marketing vice president commissioned a study to determine why the company's line-extension strategy wasn't working. The study revealed that the line extensions actually reduced sales and market share to some extent by crowding out the most popular items to make room for the new products.

In competitive markets, where shelf space was most constrained, the problem was especially acute. Random store checks revealed that the most popular items were out of stock between 5% and 50% of the time. The research showed that up to 40% of Snackco's customers deferred purchases or bought competitors' products if their favorite Snackco product was unavailable, while the remainder chose from the Snackco selections still in stock. It also projected that by recovering half the volume lost from customers who deferred purchases or switched brands, Snackco could increase its sales volume by as much as 10%.

The figures prompted Snackco's senior managers to develop a new product-line strategy. First, the company used consumer tracking panels to classify products by both household purchases and usage frequency. Then Snackco divided its product line into four categories. (See the chart "Focus on Popular Products.")

Core products were determined to be those used by more than one-third of consumers and bought more than twice a year by each consuming household. This group of products accounted for 20% of the Snackco line and 70% of the line's sales volume. Snackco managers decided to adjust manufacturing and delivery schedules to ensure that these products were always in stock in both leadership and competitive markets.

Niche products were those that were bought frequently, but only by small subsegments of consumers, often concentrated in one or more geographical markets. This group accounted for 10% of the line and 10% of sales volume. Like core products, niche products were important to the households buying them. Snackco

---

Focus on Popular Products

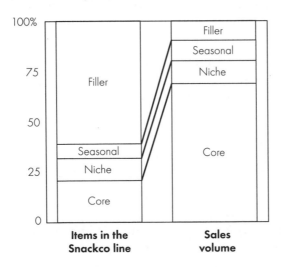

management decided to maintain them in stores where they had sufficient sales velocity but to drop them in other markets to make room for more core products.

Seasonal and holiday products were bought by more than one-third of the households but only once a year. Consumers often bought these products on impulse in addition to their core and niche selections. Items in this group represented 5% of the product line and 10% of sales volume. Management decided to continue selling these items in both leadership and competitive markets and obtain special displays during active selling periods.

Filler products accounted for the remaining 65% of the product-line items but only 10% of the sales volume. These were also purchased on impulse but had a much lower appeal than the seasonal products. When Snackco managers analyzed the hidden costs of each line extension, they found that filler items were the least profitable, even though their raw contribution margins were often higher. As a result, the managers decided to cut the number of filler products in the Snackco line to open up more shelf space for its most popular products. These cuts would be greatest in competitive markets, where Snackco would focus on building share for its core products. In leadership markets, Snackco would selectively retain filler products to defend its leadership position and block shelf space.

Snackco's managers believed that the new strategy was on target, but they also knew that without the support of the sales force, any efforts to implement the plan would fail. So, backed by Snackco's president, one of the sales regions undertook a four-month test to determine the impact of refocusing core products versus continuing line extensions. Not only did market share increase during the test, but sales-force compensation also increased because of the faster turnover of the more popular items in the line, which were given additional shelf space at the expense of the slower-moving items.

The test results generated positive word of mouth throughout the sales organization and earned the approval Snackco managers needed. The new product-line strategy was launched nationwide the following year. As added insurance, the company invested a considerable sum to train the sales force to use handheld computers that tracked individual item movement by store, thereby providing continuous evidence that the new product-line concept was succeeding.

What's more, the product-line changes were accompanied by a change in advertising strategy. Snackco shifted from an umbrella advertising approach for the whole line to a strategy that focused on its flagship products. Advertisements for these products emphasized the Snackco brand and thereby promoted the brand's line extensions. Over the past two years, Snackco has made significant gains in market share and volume, which in turn have generated even higher margins.

An Action Agenda

Like Snackco, some companies have begun to scrutinize—and rationalize—their product-line strategies. In 1992, for example, Procter & Gamble announced that it would eliminate 15% to 25% of its slower-moving SKUs over 18 months. This move represented a major turnaround from 1989 to 1990, when, over a 20-month period, the company introduced 90 new items, not one of which carried a new brand name. The reason? P&G computed the negative impact of slow movers on manufacturing and logistics costs. The company was also reacting to retailers' threats to drop slow-moving P&G SKUs. As a result of the new strategy, P&G can now close less productive plants, reduce marketing-management overhead, concentrate advertising resources on its strongest brands, and open up shelf space for genuinely new products.

Chrysler is also realizing the advantages of a more focused product line. In the late 1980s, Chrysler offered in theory over one million configurations of its cars through optional extras, even though 70% of consumers bought their cars straight off dealer lots. A look at Japanese competitors suggested an alternative approach. By offering "fully loaded" cars with far fewer options, Japanese automakers enhance manufacturing efficiency, ensure better availability and faster delivery of special orders, and reduce the risk of consumer confusion and disappointment. Chrysler is now offering fewer options on each model in a much more consumer-focused product line.

Both organizations took control of their product lines in their own fashion. But a few general rules can be drawn from their experiences. Following are eight directives that can help marketing managers improve their product-line strategies.

Improve cost accounting. Study, in detail, the absolute and incremental costs associated with the production and distribution of each SKU from the beginning to the end of the value chain. Since each SKU's costs will vary according to the volume and timing of demand, reappraise the profitability of each SKU annually or more often in the case of fashion-driven or high-technology products subject to volatile demand patterns. In companies with several hundred SKUs, focus computerized tracking systems on those items that either fall outside the bounds of acceptable profitability or are decreasing in profitability. In addition, compare the incremental sales and costs associated with adding a new SKU with the lost sales and cost savings of not doing so.

Allocate resources to winners. Sometimes budget allocations undersupport new, up-and-coming SKUs and oversupport long-established SKUs whose appeal may be weakening. As a result, managers fail to maximize marginal products. On other occasions, new line extensions that appeal only to light users may be allocated resources at the expense of core items in the franchise. Using an accurate activity-based cost-accounting system combined with an annual zero-based appraisal of each SKU will ensure a focused product line that optimizes the company's use of manufacturing capacity, advertising and promotion dollars, sales-force time, and available retail space.

Research consumer behavior. Make an effort to learn how consumers perceive and use each SKU. Core items often have a long-standing appeal to loyal heavy users. Other items generally reinforce and expand usage among existing customers. A company may need a third set of SKUs to attract new customers or to persuade multibrand users to buy from the same line more often. By carefully analyzing scanner panel data, managers can identify which SKUs in a product line substitute for or complement the core products. They can also use the data to explore price elasticities and how demand for one SKU decreases if the relative prices of other SKUs decline.

It is also critical to look at brand loyalty as a long-term behavior. Tracking panels can help companies understand their customers' habits and patterns in using their products. Then, companies can be sure to build and reinforce loyalty, as opposed to disrupting it, when they introduce a new line extension.

Apply the line logic test. Every salesperson should be able to state in one sentence the strategic role that a given SKU plays in the product line. Likewise, the consumer should be able to understand quickly which SKU fits his or her needs. Mary Kay Cosmetics limits its product line to around 225 SKUs to ensure that its beauty consultants, many of whom work part-time, can explain each one clearly; no item is added unless the company removes an existing SKU from the market. By contrast, the Avon product line has 1,500 SKUs, so the company runs special promotions to focus its door-to-door salespeople on certain items.

Coordinate marketing across the line. A complex product line can become more comprehensible to salespeople, trade partners, and customers if other elements of the marketing mix are coordinated. Consider pricing, for example. Adopting a standard pricing policy for all SKUs, or at least grouping SKUs into price bands, is often preferable—albeit at a potential cost in lost margin—to pricing each SKU separately. Consumers and retailers find consistent pricing across a product line clearer and more convincing. It also makes billing easier. Color coding standard-sized packages is another way to help consumers discriminate quickly among SKUs or SKU subcategories.

Work with channel partners. Set up multifunctional teams to screen new product ideas and arrange in-store testing with leading trade customers in order to research, in advance, the sales and cost effects of adding new SKUs to a line. Armed with the test results, distributors can avoid the opportunity costs of stocking inventory and allocating shelf space to slow-moving SKUs that they will have to remove later on. Manufacturer-trade relations will improve as a result.

Expect product-line turnover. Foster a climate in which product-line deletions are not only accepted but also encouraged. Unfortunately, in many companies, removing an SKU is harder than introducing a new one. This is true for a variety of reasons: managers may lack procedures to appraise each SKU's profitability; they may lack confidence in the potential of new items to add incremental sales; they may believe that an SKU should not be deleted as long as some customers still buy it; they may consider it important to be a full-line supplier; they may believe that implementing product-line changes is harder and more expensive than changing the other elements of the marketing mix; and they may be lulled by the ease with which promotional allowances can be used to buy shelf space and thereby cover up for a weak SKU.

Manage deletions. Once unprofitable items are identified, determine whether these items can be restored to profitability quickly and easily. Will a simple design change or a harvest strategy of raising prices and reducing marketing support do the trick? What about restricting distribution to regions or channels where the item is in heavy demand, or consolidating production of slow-moving items in a single plant designed to produce short runs of multiple products? Can costs be reduced by subcontracting production to small copackers?

If none of those approaches restores profitability, develop a deletion plan that addresses customers' needs while managing costs. For example, customers who are loyal to an item being deleted should be directed toward a substitute product. To help this process, offer a coupon that discounts both the item being deleted and the substitute. In some cases, managers may continue direct-mail delivery of an item after it is withdrawn from retail channels while customers are switched to remaining items in the line.

The costs of deleting an item include raw-material disposal, work in process, and inventories that may have to be marked down to current distributors or moved through nontraditional channels, such as warehouse clubs. The deletion plan should address how to use resources, including manufacturing capacity, freed up by the deletion. In some cases, it may make sense to launch a line extension as an existing item is removed.

THE ERA OF UNRESTRAINED line extensions is over. Improved cost-accounting systems permit manufacturers and distributors to track more accurately the comparative profitability of SKUs and the incremental costs of complexity associated with extending a product line. Increasingly powerful distributors are emphasizing "category management" and seeking to develop closer relationships with suppliers willing to organize their product lines to maximize trade profitability as well as their own. Meanwhile, consumers balk at the vast array of choices and the lack of apparent logic in many manufacturers' product lines.

Managers who focus their product lines instead of continually extending them can expand margins and market share. A controlled approach aligns products and distribution systems with customer needs, helps ensure repeat purchases, and creates stronger margins that can be reinvested in true customer value.

Originally published in September–October 1994
Reprint 94509

The Logic of Product-Line Extensions

PERSPECTIVES FROM THE EDITORS

Executive Summary:

IN THE LAST TEN YEARS, products have proliferated in every category of consumer goods and services, and the deluge shows few signs of letting up. Most companies are pursuing product expansion categories—in particular line extensions—full steam ahead. But as John Quelch and David Kenny argue in "Extend Profits, Not Product Lines" (September–October 1994; see previous article), evidence indicates that such aggressive tactics can be hazardous. Quelch and Kenny offer several guidelines for avoiding the pitfalls of wanton line extensions and sharpening product line strategies: improve cost accounting, allocate resources to popular products, research consumer behavior, coordinate marketing efforts, work with channel partners, and foster a climate in which product-line deletions are encouraged.

Nine experts offer their views on product-line management and the logic of line extensions. Some excerpts:

"In many markets, the development of product-line extensions is a competitive reality. As product categories evolve, a company must continuously adapt its product line."
    —BRUCE G. S. HARDIE AND
    LEONARD M. LODISH

"Marketers would do better if they thought of themselves as biologists studying the evolution of a species rather than as accountants studying each element of cost."
    —DAVID R. BEATTY

"As they consider new products and services, managers must carefully evaluate not only how the brand affects the line extension but also how the line extension affects the brand."
    —LAURA S. WICKE

I N THE LAST TEN YEARS, products have proliferated in every category of consumer goods and services, and the deluge shows few signs of letting up. Most companies are pursuing product-expansion strategies—in particular, line extensions—full steam ahead. But as John A. Quelch and David Kenny argue in "Extend Profits, Not Product Lines" (September–October 1994; see previous article), more and more evidence indicates that such aggressive tactics can be hazardous.

The authors see several reasons why companies rely on line extensions as part of their marketing strategies: managers perceive extensions as a low-cost, low-risk way to meet the needs of various customer segments; line extensions can satisfy consumers' desires by providing a wide variety of goods under a single brand; and managers often use extensions as a short-term competitive weapon to increase a brand's control over limited shelf space.

But for all the perceived benefits, the authors warn, the costs of wanton line extensions are dangerously high. The strategic role of each product, for example, becomes muddled when a line is oversegmented. Furthermore, a company that extends its line risks undermining brand loyalty. Line extensions rarely expand category demand, and retailers can't provide more shelf space to a category just because there are more products. Most important, the costs of overextension can remain hidden.

To avoid these pitfalls, Quelch and Kenny offer several guidelines for sharpening product-line strategies: improve cost accounting, allocate resources to popular products, research consumer behavior, coordinate marketing efforts, work with channel partners, and foster a climate in which product-line deletions are supported. As the authors illustrate in a case study, "Snackco's Fall and Rise," companies that focus a product line can increase profits and sales volume.

Nine experts offer their views on product-line management and the logic of line extensions.

BRUCE G. S. HARDIE, *Assistant Professor of Marketing, London Business School, London, England*

LEONARD M. LODISH, *Samuel R. Harrell Professor, Professor of Marketing, The Wharton School, Philadelphia, Pennsylvania, Corporate Director, Information Resources, Chicago, Illinois*

John Quelch and David Kenny's article is an excellent discussion of why cost accounting and marketing go hand in hand. We're afraid, however, that it may leave the impression that product-line extensions are all bad and should be sharply curtailed. While this may be true for many companies, it need not be true for all. Indeed, with the right cost-accounting and market-research systems in place, line extensions can be quite profitable.

Sales of the entire Doritos line of corn chips, for example, rose to more than $1 billion on the success of the Cool Ranch Doritos extension. In addition, diet and caffeine-free line extensions have expanded the soft-drink market to new segments; and the two- and three-liter bottles have stimulated consumption because, in many households, if they're in the refrigerator, they get consumed.

In many markets, the development of product-line extensions is a competitive reality. As product categories evolve, a company must continuously adapt its product lines.

In the automobile industry, the Ford Explorer and the Chrysler minivan have forged profitable new market segments that are synergistic with the older ones.

Moreover, in many markets, the development of product-line extensions is a competitive reality. As product categories evolve, a company must continuously adapt its product lines to changing market, competitive, and trade-intermediary conditions. Could Crest and Colgate have ignored the threat from Arm & Hammer's baking-soda toothpaste? During the 1980s, pump packages were must-haves; today they have all but disappeared. In 1992, Colgate introduced its stand-up tube; now it seems that all the major brands have adopted such packaging. The list goes on.

Quelch and Kenny note how improvements in supply-side information facilitate the management of product lines. Equally important, however, is demand-side information. Through the careful use of market research, product managers need to answer such questions as: How much cannibalization can we expect if we launch this line extension? Will we see greater sales if we launch this product as a line extension? How many customers will we lose if we drop this stock-keeping unit (SKU)? Cultivating such information is not a simple or cheap exercise. In our own experience, even a "simple" task like using scanner data to measure cannibalization is not as straightforward as it may seem.

Quelch and Kenny advise allocating "resources to winners"—in other words, using zero-based budgeting to allocate advertising and promotion dollars, sales-force time, and retail space. Determining the long-term and short-term profit impact of advertising and promotion requires much testing, experimentation, and analysis. Designing such programs and analyzing their results is a sophisticated, difficult activity that demands expertise.

Without a doubt, excellent market research and analysis have great influence on corporate profitability. Yet most corporations do not give these functions the recognition, visibility, or compensation they deserve. Companies need to reward their analysts based on their long- and short-term profit returns in relation to their costs. A successful product-line extension depends on investing in the appropriate cost-accounting systems and the appropriate market-research systems. (See "John Quelch and David Kenny Respond" at the end of this article.).

JAMES V. KILMER, *President, Remlik Foods, Uniontown, Pennsylvania*

Quelch and Kenny illustrate only one among many brand and product-line strategies that result from poor decision making. I wish the authors had examined another common bad habit—that of making brand decisions based on concerns with ego, money, and power, not on long-term objectives like profitability.

Ego has driven managers to proliferate brand names across categories and industries. This can lead to significant complications. For example, a brand like Weight Watchers—which spans weight-loss services, books, magazines, and foods—finds that the only common position applicable to the brand is the brand name itself. Healthy Choice, Kraft, and Heinz are among many brands competing in numerous food categories with little attention paid to building brand loyalty. Shoppers who strongly prefer Heinz in the catsup category will still choose Gerber in the baby food category. Brand recognition, the watchword of marketers today, bolsters the egos of many senior managers at the expense of brand loyalty.

Money—bonuses, stock options, and salaries—drives short-term decisions. Quelch and Kenny note that managers have set aside long-range planning and ignored the weakening of brand loyalty in favor of appeasing the financial community's demand for short-term results. But the authors fail to highlight that management directly benefits from incentive plans based on short-term goals. "Worry about achieving this quarter's goals this quarter, and worry about next quarter's goals next quarter" is the dominant sentiment expressed in many management meetings. Managers who view their tenure nearsightedly see line extensions as their opportunity for immediate personal financial gain.

Power, of course, makes managers feel more in control. Manufacturers feel that the "increasingly powerful retailers" (as Quelch and Kenny put it) are to blame for their low margins and shifting market shares. Yet these symptoms are just another consequence of avoiding long-range brand issues. Quelch and Kenny need to identify the power struggle that is being waged today between manufacturers and retailers.

When manufacturers weaken brand loyalty through their own actions, they fall prey to the retailer's desire to gain greater power in negotiations over shelf space. The power shift means greater opportunity for retailers to demand higher slotting fees and gain a larger share of profit margins. This shift will ultimately damage the egos and finances of many senior managers.

As long as manufacturers focus on the short term, profits will decline. However, guided by long-term planning, managers will make decisions that build brand loyalty and, ultimately, the power, money, and ego of those daring enough to take the long view.

DAVID R. BEATTY, *President, Weston Foods Ltd., Toronto, Ontario, Canada*

Marketers would do better if they thought of themselves as biologists studying the evolution of a species rather than as accountants studying each element of cost in ever finer detail. Biomarketing—when marketers adopt an evolutionary perspective—will save today's market leaders from becoming dinosaurs.

Just as in biological niches, where inhabitants constantly compete for resources and mutate over time, cereals, soft drinks, and other goods change and evolve. "Parent" products like Pepsi give rise to evolutionary "children" like diet sodas.

In addition to gradual evolution, "punctuated equilibrium" also exists in both ecological and marketing realms. Dramatic shifts in the environment force great bursts of change. Just as a natural cataclysm wiped out

the dinosaurs 65 million years ago, a technological cataclysm eliminated the horse and buggy 100 years ago. The
biomarketer must constantly research the environment
and the vagaries of each population, looking not only for
the gradual mutations but also for the bursts of change.
Failure to adapt product lines to either of these types of
change means extinction.

Such environmental shifts are now changing the
dynamics of packaged goods. For more than 50 years,
manufacturers have been the dominant industry
force, garnering most of the economic surplus.
But today the NYSE-listed packaged-goods
companies that have lost more than $50 billion in
market value since Marl-boro Friday are in danger of being overwhelmed by the
new retailer speciation.

Marketers would do better if they thought of themselves as biologists studying the evolution of a species rather than as accountants studying each element of cost.

Retailers are taking control of their shelves and their
customers. Consider the growth of store labels, such as
President's Choice and Sam's American Choice. These
labels offer a product as good as or superior to the
national brand leader at prices 30% to 50% below the
leader's price. Store labels like these have created a sud-
den burst of change. Those who don't respond vigor-
ously will be wiped out.

In the cookie category, which grew a modest 2% in
1993, Nabisco has introduced a full line of Fat Free Fruit
Bars and its new Snackwell line. These new "species" of
offerings have so appealed to U.S. consumers that
Nabisco's sales have increased three times as fast as the
overall market. Nabisco has prospered as its branded

competitors have withered precisely because of its product-line innovation.

Diversifying the product line, creating new products, and splitting large stock-keeping units into smaller ones both ensure that the parent brand will evolve to meet the demands of consumers and make it much tougher for the retailer to supplant the species with a store label.

There are many dead ends in product-line evolution as well as in species evolution. These dead ends are indeed costly. And there are marginal players who hang on by their fingernails. But the essence of life and products is change. Biomarketers must innovate.

PAUL W. FARRIS, *Landmark Communications, Professor of Business Administration, The Darden Graduate School of Business Administration, The University of Virginia, Charlottesville, Virginia*

Quelch and Kenny provide a timely summary of the reasons and rationalizations for product proliferation. My own shelf-space research, in fact, leads me to support their analysis of Snackco. I do, however, see a role for extensions as a method of continually improving the core brand.

Shelf-allocation models that two colleagues and I built confirm that selecting the right products and giving them enough space to keep them in stock are far more important than adding space for marginal items. Shelf-management systems that do not consider how consumers behave when products are out of stock mislead marketers and retailers into adding more product lines than they really need.

The problem Snackco faces can become an even tougher battle in the majority of companies. First, other companies generally depend on secondary market-research suppliers for shelf data. Second, other companies have only indirect influence on the shelf, mainly through retail buyers and merchandisers. Snackco's direct-delivery system supplies good data and greater influence over how products are placed.

Deciding which products are core is the sticky point. Simply replacing established brands with new, improved formulas can be unnecessarily risky.

Third, because Snackco delivers directly to stores, it may economically place lower quantities on the shelf. Other companies have to deal with the minimum-order quantities dictated by more cumbersome delivery systems, further reducing the flexibility of shelf designs. These factors argue for other companies to stick even closer to their core products.

Deciding which products are core is the sticky point. Simply replacing established brands with new, improved formulas can be unnecessarily risky. New Coke (more recently known as Coke II) is a prime example of a "better" product that encountered unexpected resistance. On the other hand, Diet Coke was the most successful soft-drink introduction for decades. Contrary to the predictions of some positioning gurus, it beat Tab cold. Perhaps Coke II would have been more successful if the company had initially given consumers a choice between formulas. Product-line extensions can be effective ways to test-market product improvements and at the same time address emerging segments.

A new brand may often be the best way to market genuinely new products. For example, it is hard to say whether Diet Coke was the best way to introduce low-calorie soft drinks. Even if the new brand succeeds, however, its niche may develop into a strong market segment. Then established brands may be forced to introduce similar extensions to fight competition. Sanka pioneered the decaffeinated coffee category, but time and the popularity of reduced caffeine have forced all major brands to make decaffeinated versions of their own.

This system, which produces duplication, also encourages brands to innovate or be left behind. A company therefore must regularly pare the product and brand lineup to give others a chance. That is the spirit in which I interpret Quelch and Kenny's suggestions for steering a course between variety and redundancy.

ALEXANDER L. BIEL, *President, Alexander L. Biel & Associates, Mill Valley, California*

Much of Quelch and Kenny's well-crafted thesis on the danger of wanton brand extension is based on the extremely tough retail environment for fast-moving consumer goods. In my view, the real danger in unbridled, unstrategic brand extension is the dissipation of brand image—a hazard not limited to packaged goods. However, there is also a very real opportunity to use line extensions to build a positive image for the parent brand.

The image of a brand arguably drives its equity. Conventional wisdom suggests that advertising is invariably the source of brand image. But, in fact, brand extensions can fundamentally change the image of the parent brand.

If the fit is inappropriate, the extension can do substantial harm. Well managed, however, it can be an enormous benefit. For example, when Mercedes-Benz launched the 190 model in the mid-1980s, the company was able to reach farther down into the sub-luxury-buyer segment than ever before. The risk: Would the 190 degrade the image of the established Mercedes brand? On the contrary, the introduction contributed an excitement and youthfulness to the entire line.

Think of brand image in terms of three components: maker image, product image, and user image. Mercedes could have chosen a safer route by introducing a new brand positioned as "by Mercedes." Although a costly strategy, it would have leveraged the maker image while insulating it from any possible degradation associated with a less prestigious car. However, this strategy would have limited the attractive user image that the Mercedes 190 quickly developed and donated to the parent brand.

Similarly, introducing an upscale line can be a useful strategy for a marketer with a downscale image. When Gallo introduced its premium varietals, the company decided to use the Gallo brand name. Gallo's prior association with lower price points clearly reduced the appeal of the new varietal line. But the upmarket product image, in addition to the user image of the varietals, was an important positive association for the parent. In other words, the varietals serve a useful purpose beyond their own volume contribution.

When Gallo came out with wine coolers, on the other hand, the company wisely distanced itself by building a separate brand, Bartles & Jaymes. While the Gallo brand name could have helped create consumers' acceptance of this product, the wine cooler's soft-drink image too strongly contradicted the brand-enhancement strategy of the wines.

Without a doubt, the cost of line-extension failures can be great. The inadequacies of Apple's Newton, for example, cast a shadow of doubt on the company's core competencies. But even when line extensions fail, they don't necessarily damage their parents fatally. Consumers are often willing to forgive strong brands when they stumble. What's more, failed extensions are usually withdrawn sooner rather than later, giving them less time to do damage.

Brand extension is a double-edged sword. Even a successful extension can damage its parent's image. However, the strategic use of extensions can also help reshape the image of the parent brand.

LAURA S. WICKE, *Senior Partner, Marketing Corporation of America, Westport, Connecticut*

Add to Quelch and Kenny's risks of line extensions the risk of diluting a brand's equity dramatically with multiple line extensions. As they consider new products and services, managers must carefully evaluate not only how the brand affects the line extension but also how the line extension affects the brand.

A brand's equity consists of the key elements that drive demand for brand products and services. This includes *some* aspects of how customers perceive and experience the brand—its image—but not necessarily *all* aspects. It is critical to identify the key equity elements and to ensure that the line-extension strategy is appropriately

As they consider new products and services, managers must carefully evaluate not only how the brand affects the line extension but also how the line extension affects the brand.

designed to leverage, protect, and reinforce the brand equity. Consistency with brand image may not be enough; consistency with the brand equity is required.

If the line-extension image jars with any of the brand equity elements, it will erode the entire line. For example, a major producer and marketer of fresh premium branded meats developed a series of processed-meat line extensions. The company hoped to leverage its "high quality" image, which it believed to be its essential brand equity. Unfortunately, its equity was more strongly related with "freshness"—an image at odds with processed food. The company ultimately withdrew the product-line extensions. But had managers measured the profitability of the line extensions alone, they would have continued to market the products with potentially disastrous consequences for the core brand product lines.

Multiple line extensions that weaken a brand's identity can also erode equity. A leading manufacturer of upscale men's and women's casual wear learned this the hard way. The company extended a strong brand name associated with an upscale, leisured lifestyle across a broad range of apparel. The brand name lost value quickly, ultimately damaging the success of both the parent and the line extensions.

A final critical consideration is the parent company's long-term mission for the brand. Given the costs highlighted in the article, it is more necessary than ever to extend only those products that will advance the brand in the appropriate strategic direction. Consider the experience of a major materials company, which had a branded home-improvement product with line-extension opportunities in several markets, including do-it-yourself, retail, wholesale, and institutional markets. Only when the company identified the brand's equity and focused its efforts did the marketing department have the direction it needed to plan strategic product-line extensions.

An appropriate line-extension strategy for a brand requires the discipline to evaluate the true costs, in terms of both immediate economic considerations and long-term impact on brand equity. The managers of a successful brand must develop a clear understanding of its key equity elements and implement guidelines for leveraging them in the marketplace. If each line extension reinforces the brand's equity, there is a greater chance of extending loyalty.

JOHN B. BALSON, *President and CEO, Sandhill Group, Jupiter, Florida*

I have long doubted the marketing wisdom of most product-line extensions, which seem doomed to fail for one simple reason: they serve manufacturers' needs rather than those of consumers. However, I believe that we can better define the overall marketing circumstances that explain the difference between success and failure in line-extension efforts.

Failures in line extensions come in all shapes and sizes. They include forgettable items like light whiskeys and more notable failures like Pepsi Clear and McDonald's pizza, which made little sense to consumers and had almost nothing in common with the image or benefits of the parent brands. I would argue that even some of the most publicized line-extension products, such as Miller Lite and Diet Coke, have done considerable long-term volume and market-share damage to their parent products. It is not inconceivable that Coca-Cola and Miller might have even larger corporate consumer franchises today had they invested in new brands rather than in product-line extensions.

Major product-line extensions often breed paranoia in marketers. Questions concerning benefits, target audiences, and levels of support for the centerpieces of a line become almost impossible to resolve. All major items usually suffer in this situation because managers decide what to push based on their fear of cannibalization rather than on consumer response.

On the other hand, product-line extensions can work when they adhere to a well-thought-out strategy. The disinfectant Lysol, for example, proved that a brand can be extended across several categories—if a common and important consumer benefit exists in both the products and consumer perceptions. I call this line-extension strategy "common benefit exploitation." Lysol was the gold standard in killing germs—a benefit with widespread household applications. Thus, Lysol was able to market products in several additional household-cleaning categories without sacrificing volume or share for the parent brand.

Line extensions can also increase a brand's consumer share of requirements within a given product category— a strategy I call "real variety need fulfillment." In the wine business, the varietal product line made by Mondavi is a perfect example of this strategy. Given the proclivity of heavy wine drinkers to seek variety in their varietal wine choice, it makes sense for Mondavi to offer a range of consistently high-quality varietals to increase the brand's share of requirements. (My one caveat is that the marketer must build enough volume to offset the shelf-space, manufacturing, and distribution cost inefficiencies discussed in the article.)

Whether or not to extend a product line is, above all, a matter of common sense. At a bare minimum, an extension must pass the simple tests of consumer benefit, share-of-requirements growth, brand image, longevity, and activity-based profits. Even then, be careful. The need for short-term volume and profits can lead to long-term problems.

DAVID A. AAKER, *Professor, Haas School of Business, University of California, Berkeley, California*

As Quelch and Kenny observe, there are risks associated with line extensions, many of which are unforeseen, underestimated, or ignored. But there are legitimate reasons for line extensions in addition to those mentioned by the authors.

Energizing a brand. A line extension can be a way to make a brand more relevant, interesting, and visible. In doing so, it can create a basis for differentiation, build the audience for the advertising of a tired brand, and stimulate sales. Consider Hidden Valley Honey Dijon Ranch salad dressing, which revitalized a tired though healthy brand. New and old customers had a new reason to use Hidden Valley.

Expanding a brand's core promise for new users. A brand may have a strong image that promotes loyalty but is exclusionary. A line extension can expand that promise. Honey Nut Cheerios, for example, provided Cheerios entry for those who bought presweetened cereals. In a similar way, the explosion of low-fat or nonfat line extensions breaks down barriers to many users.

Managing true innovation. Line extensions can be a way to foster and manage innovation, thereby enhancing the value proposition, expanding the usage contexts, and blocking competitive options. Glade Air Fresheners started with aerosols and added solid forms for continuous freshening, clip-ons for the car, and a variety of more pleasing forms.

Blocking or inhibiting competitors. Although niche markets may represent marginal businesses, they may strategically represent important footholds for competitors. Line extensions have the potential of inhibiting or neutralizing competitor moves. Recall the horrible results when General Motors, Xerox, and other companies permitted Japanese companies to gain a toehold at the low end of their respective industries because the returns did not meet the financial criteria.

Managing a dynamic environment. Line extensions provide a way to survive in an environment full of ambiguous and transitory signals and forces. General Mills faces a risk in creating a new cereal fortified with beta-carotene and vitamin E. But it also faces the risk that such a segment may be a precursor to a larger trend that, if ignored, might generate a strategically altered landscape with a first-mover competitor holding a considerable advantage. Imagine if an analysis of line-extension costs, as suggested by Quelch and Kenny, inhibited Chrysler from introducing the minivan, which, by all accounts, has saved the company.

John Quelch and David Kenny Respond: "Extensions must be carefully planned and monitored."

WE ARE PLEASED THAT, in large part, the respondents agree that the careful management of line extensions is a vital issue. Unfortunately, a few of the participants misinterpreted our argument. Bruce Hardie and Leonard Lodish, for example, wrote that our article "may leave the impression that product-line extensions are all bad and should be sharply curtailed." This is most definitely not the case. We state in our article that line extensions can be strategically sound and extremely profitable. Our emphasis was, and is, that such extensions must be carefully planned and monitored. Poorly planned, excessive extensions can be dangerous. Our message is not a call for the end to line extensions but a caution against their unbridled use.

With an understanding of our argument, several of the respondents offered valuable additional analysis and commentary. David Aaker and others pointed out that line extensions can reinforce or rejuvenate a brand's image and enhance brand equity among current and potential users. Line extensions can also block the entry opportunities for competitors or raise the price of admission.

While our focus was on the hidden costs of line extensions, several respondents, including Laura Wicke, emphasized how poorly planned line extensions can incrementally diminish a brand's equity without this effect being noticed until it is too late. Alexander Biel correctly pointed out that consumers can forgive and forget if weak line extensions are withdrawn promptly. However, as John Balson observed, many companies lack the motivation and the cost data needed to separate the successes from the failures clearly, and few prune their product lines as aggressively as they add to them.

Paul Farris correctly underlined our goal of helping companies steer "a course between variety and redundancy." As David Beatty noted, the politics of brand-management career paths and the need to preserve shelf facings in view of the higher quality private-label competition result in too many line extensions being launched in the hope that one or two will stick. The accompanying oversegmentation and a lack of logic in the product line inevitably diminishes a supplier's credibility with the trade.

The frequency of line extensions is often a better measure of a company's desperation than of its innovativeness. Constant pressure for the next line extension reduces the resources available for significant new product development. Many companies find it hard to persuade their best managers to take the career risk involved in working on a big new product idea for two to three years. At the same time, some new product ideas that, if properly nurtured, could be launched as significant entries are hijacked by managers of existing brands and marketed suboptimally as line extensions.

A marketer's imagination should not be constrained by an excessive focus on either cost control or scanner data. Such focus can greatly inhibit the marketer's ability to conceive and bring to market the breakthrough new products that can change the face of a product category. We continue to believe, however, that marketers should be more disciplined in adding only those extensions that enhance a brand's equity, have a clear strategic purpose, and, finally, add to a brand's profitability.

Originally published in November–December 1994
Reprint 94607

Can This Brand Be Saved?

REGINA FAZIO MARUCA

Executive Summary

CAROLINE PORTAL KNOWS that La Shampoo is in trouble. Introduced in 1975 and targeted at women between the ages of 15 and 30, La Shampoo had a stylish image that had immediately become popular. Its slogan, "La Shampoo: For the Look and Feel of France," had remained the same since day one. In 1989, however, the line had begun a slow descent, but the company hadn't really addressed the problem until two years ago, when it named Caroline brand manager.

At first, Caroline requested a new packaging design. The ad agency backed her up and called for a modest "new look" campaign. But the repackaging caused tension in the office and had no positive effect on sales: the numbers continued their slow decline. Caroline calls a meeting to examine proposals submitted by product

147

sales manager Eric Woolf and a representative of the ad agency that held the La Shampoo account, Beth Hanson. Eric recommends a price cut, while Beth wants a relaunch. The tension grows in the meeting as Caroline weighs the options. A decision has to be made soon in order to save the brand.

Which marketing plan should Caroline choose? Five experts examine the challenges of rebuilding a brand.

I T WAS ALMOST 11 P.M. when Caroline Portal left the office. She was exhausted. The day had been filled with one meeting after another, and she wanted nothing more than to crawl into bed and get some sleep. But she couldn't head home before stopping by the local 24-hour supermarket. The store was enormous— 18 aisles of food, pharmaceuticals, stationery, and books, even small appliances. Squinting in the bright lights, Caroline made her way to the health-and-beauty aisle and stood, staring, at the display of La Shampoo on the top shelf. Nearby, grouped with other conditioners, was the La Shampoo conditioner.

Introduced in 1975 and targeted at women between the ages of 15 and 30, La Shampoo had a stylish image that had immediately become popular. The line had quickly advanced from a strong West Coast regional presence to a solid 4% share of the national market—a position it had held more or less steadily for 14 years. La Shampoo's basic products and packaging had been modified several times over the years, but its look had remained essentially unchanged. And its slogan, "La

Shampoo: For the Look and Feel of France," had stayed
the same since day one. In 1989, the line had begun a
very slow descent, but the company hadn't really
addressed the problem until two years ago, when it
named Caroline brand manager.

At first, Caroline called for a new packaging design.
She knew that La Shampoo was in trouble, but maybe a
quick pick-me-up would do the trick. The ad agency
backed her up and developed a modest "new look" campaign. This repackaging had caused a lot of tension at
the office. Most of the people who worked on La Shampoo had been with the company for years and couldn't
imagine anything other than a slight variation on the
tall, slim, blue plastic bottles with the beige labels and
cursive lettering. And, in fact, the repackaging—a wider
bottle and yellow label with sharper lettering—had had
no positive effect on sales since its introduction eight
months ago: the numbers had continued their slow
decline. Caroline wondered if many customers had even
noticed the change.

Caroline shifted her gaze down to the products displayed at eye level. All newer than La Shampoo. All
starting to grab market share. But with no consistent
recipe for success—at least none that she could discern.
Some claimed to be "green" products, charged a premium, and made out like bandits. One touted a "Low,
Low, Low Price!" and sold huge quantities. La Shampoo
had always been a high-quality product, a bit more
expensive than its competitors, and its marketing strategy—other than the package redesign—had remained
consistent over the years. La Shampoo had always sold
on an image of European mystique. Clearly, though, that
message wasn't working anymore. Bleary-eyed, Caroline

left the health-and-beauty aisle and walked slowly toward the exit, deep in thought.

T HE NEXT MORNING, Caroline was at her desk early, doing some last-minute prep work for an 8 A.M. marketing meeting with Eric Woolf, her product sales manager, and Beth Hanson, a representative of the advertising agency that held the La Shampoo account. Both had submitted proposals before the meeting; each document was thoughtfully constructed and presented a cogent argument. (See the interoffice memos at the end of this article.) However, the two recommendations were radically different. Beth thought that La Shampoo needed a strong brand campaign. Eric wanted to compete on price. Caroline wasn't convinced either of them had the right recipe, but she did feel strongly that the middle road wasn't an option.

At the meeting, Eric spoke first. "I'm not going to waste anyone's time mincing words. We need a short-term solution as well as a long-term plan. Some of our key accounts are in jeopardy, and the only way to save them is to lower our prices permanently."

"That's not a real solution," Beth countered. "What happens after you cut the price? The competing brands will lower their prices, too, and then we'll be in the same situation we're in now."

"You don't seem to be getting the point, Beth," Eric snapped. "La Shampoo is dead unless we discount right now. We need to buy some time in order to save the brand."

Caroline raised her eyes toward the ceiling but said nothing. Eric was known for getting riled up pretty quickly, and today, it seemed, was no exception. His style worked for revving up his sales force, but it didn't go over as well in a small conference room.

"And you don't seem to understand that you won't be buying any time by making that kind of move," Beth shot back. "If you drop the price, you won't have a brand left to build up."

Eric stood up and grabbed a black marker. He quickly outlined a bar graph on the wall board depicting national market-share levels of the top shampoo brands and then circled the bar representing La Shampoo, just below the 3% mark.

"Here is where we are," he said. He drew another circle below and to the right of the first one. "Here is where we'll be in three months without some sort of price advantage." He jabbed at the board, crushing the marker's felt tip. "I'm telling you, we don't have the time to develop and roll out a completely new ad campaign. After we've stabilized the account, maybe. But not now. I'm even beginning to think that trying to protect any kind of brand name is a losing battle. You've read the papers—brands are going the way of the dinosaur."

"You're too close to the issue to see what's good for the product," Beth said.

"And you're too concerned with your own interests," Eric countered. "At bottom, you want a new advertising campaign because it will be good for your company."

The debate went around in circles. After a mere 25 minutes, Caroline could see that discussion of this kind wouldn't solve anything. She called the meeting to a halt.

"I'm going to have to review your proposals again and come to a decision," she said. "I'd like a commitment from each of you that you'll support the plan I choose, even if it is not yours. You both know that the only way either of these options will work is if we pull together at every level—and those of us at the top will have to send that message."

Beth nodded. "I'll support that," she said.

Eric stood up. "I will as well," he said. "But if you're seriously considering a new advertising campaign, I think you'll find out pretty quickly that we're too late for that kind of move." He gathered his papers and quickly left, letting the door slam shut behind him.

Caroline was temporarily at a loss for words. She hadn't expected Eric to leave so abruptly. She told Beth that she'd get back to both of them within a week and followed Eric into the hall, but he was already gone.

Back in her office, Caroline returned a few phone calls and then turned her attention to her E-mail. She had only one message—from Marni Shin, director of new product development.

"Caroline, I'd like to schedule a meeting with you ASAP to discuss the combination shampoo/conditioner our team has been working on. We should have a pre-liminary conversation about La Shampoo, and whether or not you think our new combo should be rolled out as part of the La Shampoo line. I think it should. Our research indicates that people are increasingly demand-ing more convenient products like combos. Without some kind of a shot in the arm, La Shampoo will be at the end of its life cycle sooner than we'd all like to think. And, frankly, it will be an embarrassment to the com-pany if we don't introduce a combo soon. We've been ready for four months."

"As if I didn't have enough to deal with," Caroline said under her breath. The market research was so cloudy that it could be used to support almost any argu-ment. And Caroline had heard Marni talk about new product launches before. Marni clearly had no concept of what was needed to build a brand. But Marni's limitations weren't the issue right now. La Shampoo was the problem, and some decision about the marketing plan had to be made soon.

Which marketing plan should Caroline choose?

Five experts examine the challenges of rebuilding a brand.

CAROL ALLMAN *is the director of merchandise at the Eckerd Drug Company, a chain of drugstores based in Largo, Florida.*

I'd hate to be the sales rep for La Shampoo when he makes his next call at my company. He has probably done a lot of talking already in an attempt to keep the product in our stores. And I'm sure that when La Shampoo was repackaged, he tried his best to convince us that the new look would turn the brand around. But here it is eight months later, and the customers haven't even blinked. We're not about to welcome him with open arms.

In fact, unless he has a new product launch in his back pocket or some convincing market-research data showing substantially improved market share, he might as well stay at home. As things stand, there doesn't seem to be a good financial reason for any retailer to continue to maintain distribution. Shelf space is expensive, and it doesn't sound like La Shampoo is generating enough sales potential to pay the rent.

Don't get me wrong—the account rep is doing his job. As a retailer, our reluctance to continue stocking La

Shampoo would most likely have nothing to do with him. But, at this point, the sales staff needs some direction from the brand manager to justify La Shampoo's positioning. Chances are that there are at least three other salespeople sitting in our lobby with products that can easily claim the shelf space currently occupied by La Shampoo. And today the clock is ticking much faster than it used to. Gone are the days when retailers would let a product or line of products eat up a year or two of shelf distribution while brands were repositioned, repackaged, and relaunched. Retailers are now able to forecast individual stock-keeping-unit (SKU) performance on a monthly basis and forecast sales potential of any new item under consideration. As a result, they're much less patient with underperforming brands.

The burden is on Caroline Portal to save the brand, and she needs to act quickly. These days, brand managers can afford a grace period of only about six months before they must begin to make changes in or discontinue underperforming brands. Caroline's goal is to improve sales and gross profit dollars per square foot, not to maintain the status quo. Right now, she isn't even managing to do that.

Fortunately, there *is* a solution, and Caroline has the information she needs to move forward. However, neither Eric's nor Beth's recommendations were completely accurate.

Eric Woolf, for example, was right to say that the sales reps need immediate support but wrong to suggest competing on price alone. The price game will guarantee failure unless the company is prepared to support that positioning with substantial advertising and lower the price still further once other brands respond in kind. In addition, price-driven consumers have absolutely no loyalty; if La Shampoo competes on price, its support base will crumble if another brand comes along a penny cheaper, offering a benefit La Shampoo can't provide, like "salon styling at a bargain price" or "beautiful hair from natural sources."

Beth Hanson's solution was closer to the mark but still not quite there. She shouldn't have recommended a new ad campaign without suggesting a change in La Shampoo's positioning. Today's consumers are smart. A slogan like "For the Look and Feel of France" means nothing in the current retail environment, and customers won't spend their money on hype alone. They want to know what they're getting for their money. The new ad campaign should focus on benefits, such as healthy hair, or hair that looks good, feels good, and makes you feel good. I haven't heard people tell me lately that they want to look French.

Today's consumers don't respond to hype. They want to know what they are getting for their money.

We also know that La Shampoo's existing customer base doesn't like change, so Caroline should know better than to fool around with the formula or the bottle. Unfortunately, La Shampoo's customer base is not growing, and it will eventually die. Caroline must find some new trial and usage for the brand. Enter Marni with the last piece of the puzzle: La Shampoo two-in-one, which will enable Caroline to tap into a new consumer base, generate additional advertising support for the brand, and protect the current La Shampoo user.

In short, Caroline must reposition the existing brand with a benefits statement that is meaningful for today's market and immediately launch the new two-in-one

product under the La Shampoo name. If a sales rep
could show me a plan like that, I would consider keeping
La Shampoo on my shelves.

SAM I. HILL *is a partner in the Sydney, Australia, office
of Booz-Allen & Hamilton, where he leads work for consumer goods and services clients in the Asia-Pacific
region. He focuses on strategic and organizational issues
in sales, marketing, and distribution. David Newkirk, a
partner in the London, England, office, and Gerard Cun-
ningham, a senior associate in Singapore, also contributed to this commentary.*

While the immediate challenge facing Caroline Portal
is coming up with a viable marketing strategy for La
Shampoo, she also needs to address a broader concern:
La Shampoo's brand management. It is very troubling
that she and her team went from symptom to surgery
without even stopping at diagnosis. This type of
approach, unfortunately employed far too often, is
labeled "Rambo" marketing, and it is easy to see why.

Still, it is an encouraging sign that Caroline ended the
meeting with Eric Woolf and Beth Hanson after only 25
minutes. Maybe she'll step back from the edge of panic
and gain some perspective before jumping to implement
a plan that in the end might hurt the product more than
it helps.

If Caroline does pause to reflect, I think she will find
that Beth's proposal is closer to the mark than Eric's. To
hold its own in the ferocious, innovation-intensive haircare category for almost two decades, La Shampoo must
have a tremendously strong brand equity. The strategic
value of brand equity is consistently underestimated and
often slighted in favor of more tangible competitive
advantages, such as technological superiority or lower
pricing. This is a fundamental mistake. Eric's argument

that La Shampoo has a loyal customer base that cares enough to resist any change should be the best news that Caroline has had all day.

The other alternatives, proposed by Marni Shin and Eric, are likely to be too little, too late. Competitors have already filled the shelves with two-in-ones and value-for-money brands. It's hard to see how "me too" strategies will reverse La Shampoo's share erosion. Nor are Marni's and Eric's strategies without risk. Either could dilute La Shampoo's positioning and alienate existing users.

But choosing Beth's plan does not mean that La Shampoo is out of the woods. The good news is that Caroline has a viable strategy. The bad news is that merely knowing the right strategy is of little use. Many managers, particularly when faced with a problem of mounting proportions, mistake action for productivity. So even if Caroline selects the "right" solution, she needs to know much more to make that strategy actually work.

Restaging a brand requires considerable resources. And La Shampoo's next move could have dramatic bottom-line impact.

First, restaging the brand will require considerable resources, and Caroline will need to pull together a case that will win over her superiors. Quite reasonably, senior management will most likely require more than anecdote, opinion, and "cloudy" market research before committing to any particular plan. This is a big decision for La Shampoo. Hair care is among the most competitive and least forgiving of categories in the supermarket. And La Shampoo's next move could have dramatic bottom-line impact. If one assumes that La Shampoo's price is average for the market, a 10% price cut would cost the brand $5 million if it is unsuccessful in recapturing significant lost share. Alternatively, a major relaunch could cost $25 million at the very least.

Second, our research has found that strategies fail for the most part because of poor execution, not because of the plans themselves. Caroline and her team do not know nearly enough about the market to design an effective plan of action. Before moving forward, they must step back and answer a fundamental set of questions about customers, competitors, and channels.

Customers. What do La Shampoo's customers think? Caroline claims that market-research results are ambiguous. This is not surprising. In our experience, market-research results are seldom anything *but* ambiguous, usually because market researchers insist on asking the wrong questions of the wrong people. The attitudes that matter are those of loyal users and former users who have—or had—a relationship with the brand.

Trying to build an effective action plan based on data developed from a random sample of all women ages 15 to 55 is probably futile. Such data will not provide Beth with the specificity of information that she needs to design an effective communications campaign. Caroline should ask herself whether the needs of a 15-year-old student living in Manhattan, New York, are likely to be the same as those of a 50-year-old teacher living in Manhattan, Kansas. Or is a 30-year-old stay-at-home mother of four from Peoria, Illinois, likely to share buying criteria with a 30-year-old single lawyer who lives in San Francisco, California? Probably not. La Shampoo's management must identify who its customers are and why they are leaving the brand.

Competitors. Who has benefited at La Shampoo's expense? A single brand or a range of products? Are the winners other premium products, lower priced brands, or two-in-ones? Has the erosion occurred gradually? Can erosion be linked to identifiable events? Obviously, different sets of implications arise depending on whether share has been lost either to two-in-ones or other premiums or to lower priced products.

Channels. What do retailers identify as the problem? With scanning technology and sophisticated information systems, today's retailer often knows as much about brand dynamics as the marketers do. Will the trade support the selected strategy? The reality is that channel support is increasingly critical to the success of any marketing initiative. For example, Eric can cut the wholesale price and the recommended retail price, but the retailer determines the actual shelf price. Similarly, Marni can develop a two-in-one, but the buying committees of major retailers reject hundreds of new products every year. If retailers believe that two-in-ones already have sufficient space allocation, La Shampoo may be wasting its time.

The need to work closely with channels is painful for most marketers. Trained to believe that the brand manager should have absolute power, they find the need to treat channels as strategic partners an unwelcome constraint. Nonetheless, they must learn to take channel relationships seriously. La Shampoo must have not only the right strategy but also a salable one.

SANDRA LAWRENCE *is the division vice president of marketing for all consumer, industrial, and technical products at Polaroid USA, based in Cambridge, Massachusetts. Formerly, she was vice president for new products and business development in the personal care division of Gillette Company.*

It seems that Caroline has forgotten a basic tenet of any successful marketing strategy: the mix. Indeed, a successful marketing strategy in any field is the result of a combination of product, price, positioning, and placement. And that combination in turn results from people in different areas working together toward a common goal.

Before Caroline makes a decision about strategy, then, she must address a few issues concerning organizational behavior. First of all, she has to find a way to persuade Beth and Eric to work together constructively. At this point in time, it's highly unlikely that any meeting among them would be either amicable or collaborative. Caroline has pitted her colleagues against each other by giving them the impression that this is an either/or situation. Instead of calling a meeting to discuss which proposal she will choose, Caroline should hold a brainstorming session. Present at the session should be representatives from research and development, manufacturing, market research, sales, as well as advertising. She can make clear at the outset that the meeting's purpose is not to determine the strategy for La Shampoo. Rather, the purpose of the meeting would be to explore the parameters and the implications of several different strategies.

What if Caroline chooses a retention strategy? Suppose she tries to keep her existing customers and accounts and introduces a new brand name to launch some of the more "modern" related products? What if Caroline decides on a new-customer-acquisition strategy using the old brand name and its residual brand equity?

The meeting's participants could then compare the cost implications of each potential strategy and assess the probability of success. The research-and-development team, in particular, could offer some enlightening information. For example, what are some

It seems that Caroline has forgotten a basic · tenet of any successful marketing strategy: the mix.

of the other new products in the works? How can a new kind of product add value to the marketplace? After such a meeting, Caroline could review the input and make a decision, knowing that all the cards had been on the table and that she had received everyone's best advice and thinking for each strategy considered.

Once the strategy issue is settled, Caroline should move ahead quickly and efficiently. Again, she needs to remember that the mix is the key to success. Packaging alone isn't enough to alter purchasing behavior, but it nonetheless leaves a lasting impression on the consumer. Smart packaging executed as part of an effective strategy can really add to the shelf power and merchandising power of a brand.

Similarly, price will not necessarily make the difference in and of itself. A product's price must follow from its strategic positioning. I have seen some very good results with premium brand names that have been positioned on price alone. However, the choice must be made with sufficient background knowledge. Of course, Caroline will have to calculate the lower-margin/higher-volume trade-offs.

I would work the hardest to ensure that the advertising campaign will truly support the brand's new initiative. I've seen more success with lower budgets and a more creative advertising campaign than with huge budgets and an uninspired campaign. But the fundamental issue is that all parties will have to rally around the same strategy. Caroline will have a hard time convincing the company's senior management to support any plan if the group is filled with dissent.

JOHN DEIGHTON *is an associate professor of marketing at the University of Chicago's Graduate School of Business. His research concerns marketing communications and the implications of new communications technologies for the future of marketing practice.*

Caroline is debating solutions before forming any fact-based opinion of the problem that La Shampoo confronts. Her brand is small and declining, but that's a vague diagnosis to base a treatment on. Her immediate concern should be to establish why the brand is so sick.

To begin to identify the problem, Caroline should try to find out which market La Shampoo really serves. When a brand's share is as low as 2% or 3% of the national market, it probably holds a larger share of a smaller niche or submarket. What is La Shampoo's niche? Perhaps it is still essentially a regional brand; perhaps certain retailers favor it; perhaps it is more popular with a certain age group or ethnic group. These are questions that her market-research files should be able to answer. Caroline will be in a strong position if she has been subscribing to a retail scanner panel or has access to some of the "frequent shopper" purchase records that major retail chains are assembling. Aggregates of individual purchasing histories can show her who uses La Shampoo and how it fits into the consumption repertoire of those who use it.

If the records show a small but solid core of loyal users who depend on La Shampoo for the major share of their shampoo requirements, then there is hope for the brand. Caroline's first priority would be to invest marketing dollars to retain this core; the second would be to find more consumers, ideally younger ones, with similar tastes who can be introduced to the brand.

If, for example, the core comprised women in rural areas of the western states, Caroline could ensure that the brand was fully distributed in that market. Then she could look for similar markets, perhaps sending Eric's team on a sales scouting trip to rural markets in the South and Southwest. In the same spirit, a profile of the core user would give Beth a target to aim at and an audience with whom to explore ways to enliven the brand.

But perhaps no core of loyal users exists. What if La Shampoo's customer franchise were dispersed among a larger group of consumers who purchased the brand only infrequently? The prognosis may still be good if La Shampoo occupies a stable place in its consumers' repertoires of brands. Caroline can invest to secure the brand's place in the rotation and seek out look-alike market niches where similar rotation patterns might be feasible.

The worst case scenario would be if Caroline found that no stable repertoire existed at all; perhaps La Shampoo drifts in and out of its users' lives under the influence of price promotions and end-of-aisle displays and at the whim of the distribution channel. In that case, the customer equity of the brand is close to zero, and Caroline will not be squandering a corporate asset if she lets Eric use the brand as trade deal fodder. Her best course of action would be to rethink the opportunities in the shampoo category from scratch and make sure her résumé is up-to-date.

Can Marni's combination shampoo-and-conditioner save the brand? When you're drowning, any out-stretched hand looks good. But Caroline would be advised to study the conditioner's franchise carefully before embracing that option. If the same customers buy both products, a combination product will kill demand for the conditioner without doing much good for the shampoo.

Brands don't die until their customers desert them. Caroline needs to scrutinize a representative sample of shampoo purchasing histories to see what kind of customer franchise La Shampoo has left. If a brand of La Shampoo's long standing can't find some evidence that at least a few customers care about it, then the name is dead and the game over.

JAMES A. HANLON *is chairman of Leaf Inc. North America, a manufacturer and distributor of confectionery and collectible sports trading cards.*

Long-term brand neglect and decline can seldom be reversed with a quick fix. In my view, neither Eric's price cuts nor Beth's new campaign alone will change the course of La Shampoo's drift.

La Shampoo seems to have a larger share of mind than share of market. By that I mean that its name recognition is high and its reputation good. But those qualities don't translate into selling power. La Shampoo has a "my mother's shampoo" kind of image—it's very dependable, but most consumers probably think it's not very exciting and not for them.

While this account is grim, it is by no means a death sentence for the brand. Twenty-year-old brands generally have staying power. Good & Plenty licorice candy, for example, has recently celebrated its 100th birthday. The brand was first introduced by the Quaker City Company of Philadelphia, Pennsylvania, then subsequently sold to the American Circle Division, the Beatrice Corporation, and finally, in 1983, to Leaf. The brand was mismarketed during several periods of its life, yet retains a strong brand identity. Choo-Choo Charlie lives in part because the brand's original foundation was solid. Today's Good & Plenty is again growing, spurred by some very aggressive marketing and new distribution as part of the Leaf Famous Favorites Peg Board Candies.

La Shampoo could enjoy a similar future. My advice to Caroline is not to choose just one proposal. The brand requires attention on more than one front.

First, embrace the new product concept and introduce a new and improved La Shampoo two-in-one in a distinctive package. Consult Marni about how to make the product "green." Then market it as such, but don't charge a higher price. Consumers like the idea of "greenness," but expect the manufacturer to pay for it.

Next, in order to buy time for the new product while clearing the shelves of the old package, give away high-value coupons, which provide a short-term lift to shelf movement and hasten the appearance of the new product.

Finally, find a contemporary spokesperson and use her in a major ad campaign. The image of "my mother's shampoo" can be changed to something like "Nancy Kerrigan's shampoo" in short order. The trick is to play on the product's long-term strengths while shifting public perception in certain key areas.

La Shampoo doesn't face an insurmountable dilemma. But the question Caroline needs to address is, can we afford this? Re-creating a product isn't a low-cost endeavor. The La Shampoo problem was not created in one year but over a period of years, and it will take sustained effort to turn around the situation.

Interoffice Memo from Beth Hanson

Re: New Advertising Campaign

The time is right to make a bold re-entry. Consider the results of our market research—in particular, the feedback we received from the focus groups. One group was made up of women in their 20s, another women from 35 to 45 years of age. We ran six different group sessions, and all indicated that brand loyalty is declining, that there is an increased tendency to switch to other brands. Those sentiments are not confined to La Shampoo. We've read the industry reports. Buying patterns are fragmented across the health-and-beauty market. Women who traditionally buy high-end cosmetics may buy bargain haircare products. Women who buy branded shampoo or hair spray and expensive fragrances often purchase drugstore makeup. In our field, so many shampoos and conditioners have been recently introduced to the market that consumers are confused. Let's take advantage of the confusion. People will become loyal to certain products again. Let's make sure we're their choice for shampoo.

Interoffice Memo from Beth Hanson p. 3

Re: New Advertising Campaign

and in response to the idea of competing on price, I ask you to consider the nitty gritty results of the group surveys. A small percentage of the focus-group members seem to believe that La Shampoo is no longer a quality product. A price cut would only encourage that perception. Part of the problem is that the quality equation seems to be shifting. La Shampoo doesn't claim any of the floral and herbal extracts that seem to define quality in today's market. We should strongly consider changing the image we want to project.

Interoffice Memo from Beth Hanson p. 4

Re: New Advertising Campaign

For the last ten years, we've had essentially the same game plan: we've run ads consistently on television and in all the major women's magazines; we've given away product samples regularly at stores that carry our line. With a new national ad campaign, La Shampoo could step into the breach and recapture its lost position. I recommend increasing magazine ads, rolling the new television campaign, and getting into billboard advertising and event sponsorship. We need to focus the entire brand campaign on reinventing the La Shampoo image.

Interoffice Memo from Eric Woolf p. 2

Without a doubt, it needs a price cut. La Shampoo has irrevocably lost its position as a major brand. It was never top drawer, but now it's clearly dropping to a second tier product. What's more, most of our customers are aging with the product, so the original La Shampoo image is no longer a good fit. At the same time, the market research tells us that these customers would object to changes in design or content. Either way, a brand campaign would only throw good money after bad. If you change the image, you lose the core market. If you keep the image, you lose the core market. We should cut our losses and stake out a position as a cheap, high-quality alternative product, position ourselves just a cut above the private labels. That's the only way we'll get through the next year without sustaining the kind of damage from which no product recovers.

Interoffice Memo from Eric Woolf p. 3

The sales staff is having a hard time keeping the accounts they have, never mind increasing orders. Our retailers aren't supporting the product the way they used to, many of them no longer give La Shampoo the same share of shelf space they did in the past. And, too often, they don't place the conditioner next to the shampoo. Our salespeople can't even say that we have a solid plan of action. You need to move on this as quickly as possible.

Originally published in September–October 1994
Reprint 94508

Your Brand's Best Strategy

VIJAY VISHWANATH AND

JONATHAN MARK

Executive Summary

CONVENTIONAL WISDOM holds that market share
drives profitability. Certainly, in some industries, such as
chemicals, paper, and steel, market share and profitability are inextricably linked. But when the authors studied
the profitability of premium brands—brands that sell for
25% to 30% more than private-label brands—in 40 categories of consumer goods, they found that market share
alone does not drive profitability.

Instead, a brand's profitability is driven by both market share and the nature of the category, or product
market, in which the brand competes. A brand's relative
market share has a different impact on profitability
depending on whether the overall category is dominated by premium brands or by value brands. If a category is composed largely of premium brands, then most

of the brands in the category are—or should be—quite profitable. If the category is composed mostly of value and private-label brands, then returns will be lower across the board.

Developing the most profitable strategy for a premium brand, then, means reexamining market share targets in light of the brand's category. That is, managers must think about their brand strategy along two dimensions at the same time. First, Is the category dominated by premium brands or by value brands? Second, Is the brand's relative market share low or high?

The authors have devised a matrix using those two dimensions to help managers map the position of any premium brand within one of four quadrants: hitchhiker, high-road brand, low-road brand, and dead-end brand. Each quadrant has different implications for a brand's profit potential. And each requires a different strategy.

During the 1970s, Procter & Gamble moved aggressively to gain market share in the coffee business. Freed from a consent decree that had restrained its ability to grow geographically, Folgers, a P&G subsidiary, came east from its western stronghold and took on Maxwell House in a clash of the coffee titans. After the dust settled, Folgers indeed had moved to a new plateau of market share—from which it has not retreated. But its victory had a decidedly bitter taste. In committing to and achieving major gains in market share through its pricing actions, P&G effectively eliminated the industry profits of the entire "roast and ground" segment—a situation that persisted until the early 1990s.

What had gone wrong? Once Folgers had achieved its goal of gaining market share, why didn't significant profitability follow? Could Folgers have known in advance that its plan wasn't necessarily the best strategic move?

We believe that the answer is yes. Conventional wisdom holds that market share drives profitability. Certainly, in some industries, such as chemicals, paper, and steel, market share and profitability are inextricably linked. But when we studied the profitability of premium brands like Folgers—brands that sell for 25% to 30% more than private-label brands—in 40 categories of consumer goods, we found some surprising results. Chief among them, we discovered, was that market share alone does not drive profitability. In fact, market share explains only about half of the differences in profitability among brands; in some categories, there is hardly any correlation at all.

Instead, a brand's profitability is driven by *both* market share *and* the nature of the category, or product market, in which the brand competes. A brand's relative market share (RMS) has a different impact on profitability depending on whether the overall category is dominated by premium brands or by value brands to begin with. That is, if a category is composed largely of premium brands, then most of the brands in the category are—or should be—quite profitable. If, on the other hand, the category is composed mostly of value and private-label brands, then returns will be lower across the board. When we compared the actual profitability of the 40 premium brands we studied with their predicted profitability, using as variables RMS and the "premium"

degree of a category, we found a strong correlation. (See
the chart "What Explains a Brand's Profitability?")

The facial-skin-care category is filled largely with premium brands, and most players earn more than 15%
pretax operating profit, or return on sales (ROS). What's
more, even brands with market share one-fifth to one-
tenth that of the category leader, Oil of Olay, have operating profits only slightly lower than Oil of Olay's. But
processed meats, in which market leader Oscar Mayer
and other premium competitors account for less than
40% of the category, are a different story. The brands
with high relative market share earn about 10% ROS;
those with low relative market share usually earn less
than 5%. The category is what makes the difference.

Developing the most profitable strategy for a premium brand, therefore, means reexamining market
share targets in light of the brand's category. In other

What Explains a Brand's Profitability?

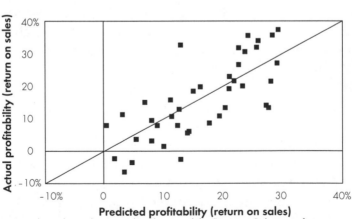

Predicted profitability (return on sales)
based on relative market share and the "premium" degree of a category

words, managers must think about their brand strategy along two dimensions at the same time. First, is the category "premium" or "value"? (Is it dominated by premium brands or by value brands?) Second, is the brand's relative market share low or high?

If we visualize a matrix with those two dimensions, we can map the position of any premium brand within one of four quadrants. Each quadrant has different implications for a brand's profit potential. And each requires a different strategy. (See the matrix "Two Dimensions, Four Strategies.")

Procter & Gamble's strategy for Folgers was based on the implicit notion that greater RMS always means greater profits. But when the company went after share, it started a price war. Competitors responded, and a category that had once been premium became value. All players suffered. Given the quadrant that Folgers had

Two Dimensions, Four Strategies

originally occupied—a market share follower in a premium category—did P&G pursue the optimum strategy?

The Hitchhiker: Premium Category, Low RMS

Folgers was what we call a *hitchhiker*. And for hitchhikers—whose average ROS is generally between 15% and 20%—gaining share by lowering prices is dangerous. Hitchhikers shouldn't rock the boat; it is usually in their best interest to follow the leader's pricing moves.

What brands in this quadrant *should* focus on is innovation coupled with niche marketing or variations on niche marketing. Successful hitchhiker brands either attract and keep a narrow base of loyal users, as Neutrogena does in the facial-bar-soap category, or lead the market in a subsegment of a larger category, as Post does in shredded-wheat and banana-nut cereals. The common theme is an innovative brand for which consumers are willing to pay a premium price.

Cereal, in fact, is a good example of a category in which the hitchhiker strategy can pay off. More than 60% of the category is made up of premium, or high-end, products, and consumers pay at least 30% more for those brands than they do for value brands, despite the recent price cuts. Kellogg is the clear market leader, but Post and General Mills each control certain subsegments and do very well following Kellogg in overall RMS.

For an interesting variation on hitchhiking, the automobile industry is worth a look. Over the past ten years, the category as a whole has become increasingly premium and profitable. Why? Automakers have figured out that it is far more rewarding to target specific customer groups with innovations—highly stylized vehicles—than to compete at the low end of the market with a high RMS. As a result, the average price of an automobile sold in the United States has risen much faster than the rate of inflation. Entire segments—such as sport utility vehicles and minivans—are continually being created and redefined; and the traditional four-door family sedan now accounts for only a small portion of the automobile category. Chrysler has been a primary driver—and the largest beneficiary—of this change. The company, which had long been a weak player in the market, now offers many niche vehicles and earns more than $1,000 in profit for each one it sells.

Brands that occupy the premium-category, low-RMS quadrant can maintain healthy profit levels for long periods. But the hitchhiker position is vulnerable—in particular to pricing moves by the market leader. If the market leader in a premium category lowers prices—as Marlboro did in the cigarette industry in 1993—the hitchhiker's profits can erode overnight, especially if the price gap between premium and value brands was wide to begin with. It's true that many premium categories sustain large price gaps for years. But managers of hitchhiker brands must recognize and evaluate the risks.

The High Road: Premium Category, High RMS

When a brand leads the market in a premium category, we call it a *high-road* brand. High-road brands generally earn more than 20% ROS. The keys to success in this quadrant are innovation, innovation, and innovation. Consumers of high-road brands tend to be loyal and willing to pay premium prices. In return, they continually demand improvements and changes—in form, size, and function—that deliver real value.

Kraft Macaroni & Cheese is a good example of a brand that has successfully sustained its position in the high-road quadrant. Building on its original product, Kraft constantly engages existing customers and attracts new ones with its innovations. For example, over the past 15 years, the company has introduced spiral pasta, pasta in the shape of cartoon characters, and several different cheese flavors—all selling at premium prices in what has remained a premium category. Clorox is another good example. Not only has it innovated in its original category, household bleaches, it has also used innovation as a way to trade on strong customer equity and to muscle into ancillary categories, such as all-purpose cleaners and toilet bowl cleaners.

Gillette is a third good example. When Gillette's main competitor introduced low-cost disposable razors sold by the bag, the dynamics of the razor category began to shift. At first, Gillette's managers responded in kind by introducing their own packages of low-cost disposable razors. Realizing, however, that a dominant share in a value-oriented category would confine the company to an ROS of 5% to 10%, they also began to consider other paths to profitability. As a result, Gillette poured more than $200 million into R&D and introduced the Sensor shaving system. The Sensor sold at a 25% price premium over Atra, another Gillette brand, which until then had been the highest-priced system on the market.

Gillette successfully made consumers "trade up" to a new spending level—and a new set of performance expectations. What's more, 15% of Sensor sales came from people who had formerly bought competitors' disposable razors. Instead of paying roughly 40 cents per razor, they began to pay $3.30 for a shaving system that

required 70-cent replacement cartridges. The Sensor and its succeeding generations of products—along with the innovations of other companies that followed suit—restored the razor category to premium status.

When managers of high-road brands are confronted with a price war or a threat from a private label, it is critical for them to think through the consequences of their reactions. Kimberly-Clark and Procter & Gamble have long faced a private-label threat to their premium products in the diaper category. Kimberly-Clark has always responded to that threat with new technologies and applications. The result? Innovations such as Ultra-trim and Pull-Ups, which allow the company to continue charging a price premium. P&G's early efforts to fight private labels, on the other hand, seemed more focused on reducing prices and repositioning its products downward. Only when that strategy failed to produce the desired results did P&G turn to innovation to sustain profitability. Pampers Baby-Dry Stretch diapers, which have a super absorbent core, and Pampers Premium diapers, which boast "breathable" side panels, are two innovations that have helped P&G strengthen its position as a high-road brand.

If innovation is the most important component of a successful high-road strategy, judicious pricing is second in importance. Educated consumers will pay more for innovation, trading up to higher-priced products. But there's a limit. Extremely high prices can produce mind-boggling returns over the short term, but such profits are not sustainable. If there is a substantial price gap between premium brands and value brands in a category, someone will fill the breach. Our research suggests that consumers are more loyal to premium brands that are only somewhat more expensive than value brands.

If there is a considerable price gap within a category, high-road brands can maintain a pricing edge for a longer time by innovating profusely. Advil's prices are 100% higher than those of equivalent private-label analgesics; but Advil's innovations have been limited, and the brand has continued to lose share to private-label offerings. Tylenol has also lost share to private-label brands, but its prolific innovation—different strengths, different forms, different formulations for specific ailments—has proved a more effective strategy than Advil's.

Raising entry barriers is the third key ingredient of a successful high-road strategy. One way to do that is through product (or stock-keeping-unit) proliferation, as Tylenol has done. Not only does such proliferation signify the brand's growth, but it also acts as a line of defense against lower-priced alternatives. Retailers would rather stock a variation on a leading brand than an alternative that cannot command proportional shelf space and hasn't been proven to turn over at a rapid rate.

Managers also can block new entrants to a category by using proprietary delivery systems, such as direct store delivery—a program through which manufacturers deliver directly to stores rather than through retailers' warehouses. If the product is perishable, a DSD program ensures freshness. DSD also gives the manufacturer enormous merchandising power. Because the person stocking the shelves is employed by the manufacturer, not only can the manufacturer control how the product is displayed, but it also knows firsthand what is selling and how fast. Programs like these tend to have high fixed costs; minor players find it difficult to respond effectively.

Coca-Cola, Frito-Lay, and Nabisco are all good examples of high-road food brands that have erected those

kinds of barriers. Frito-Lay has expanded its product line to the point where—given shelf-space constraints—competitors simply cannot keep up. What's more, its DSD system ensures that anyone who wants to compete must first confront a massive investment hurdle. Witness the demise of Eagle Snacks. Eagle simply was unable to match Frito-Lay's investments.

Finally, managers of high-road brands must be certain that their spending on support activities—such as marketing, R&D, and capital improvements—is consistent with their strategy. That's good advice in any case, but for high-road brands it is critical. Building brand equity and reinforcing the brand's image must be primary concerns; hence spending on media advertising should be a dominant part of the marketing mix. And R&D, as we've said, should focus on innovation rather than on reducing costs.

Can high-road brands fall from grace? Certainly. If managers succumb to the temptation to "milk" the brand—scaling back innovations or raising prices without offering commensurate increases in value—consumers will balk. What's more, over time such actions will reduce the premium nature of the category as a whole. Managers then will confront the twofold task of turning around a flagging brand and trying to increase profits in an area that is no longer primed to encourage higher levels of profitability.

The Low Road: Value Category, High RMS

When a brand competes in a value category and has a high RMS, we call it a *low-road brand*. Most low-road brands do not realize significant profits as a result of their price premiums; they earn an average ROS of only 5% to 10%. That's because many low-road price

premiums reflect bloated cost structures, not differentiated or more valuable products. In this quadrant,
then, the primary goal should be cutting costs and
plowing back the savings into lower prices. Managers
should take a hard look at their cost structures and
eliminate steps that do not add value. That way, they
can free up resources to devote to building brand
equity. The strategy is to encourage consumers who
are buying value brands to purchase the premium
brand by reducing the price gap between the two and
by boosting the brand's equity—in effect, giving consumers "permission" to pay the higher price.

Managers can cut costs in many areas. One option is
reducing stock-keeping units. Many low-road brands
sport large numbers of SKUs because their managers
believe that consumers value the variety. But in this
quadrant, such proliferation does not ensure greater
profits; often, it simply leads to more complex manufacturing and delivery systems, which in turn lead to higher
overhead costs. High-road brands, with their strong customer equity and their position in a premium category,
require the variety; low-road brands do not.

Other cost-cutting measures—to round up the rest of
the usual suspects—include rationalizing capacity (closing facilities), consolidating suppliers, and standardizing
components. Managers also should scrutinize the
designs of their products and packages. Over time, many
manufacturers tend to develop an almost slavish regard
for the "gold standard" and, as a result, build additional
costs into their products or packages. They need to
examine whether those extra costs are justified: do
value-oriented consumers really appreciate the additional features?

Oscar Mayer occupied the low-road quadrant in the
processed-meats business in the early 1990s and pur-

sued a low-road strategy. The company attacked costs aggressively, eliminating more than half of its SKUs, closing plants, getting out of raw-material vertical integration, and consolidating suppliers. Then it used the savings to lower prices.

Oscar Mayer benefited greatly from its strategy: over a three-year period, profits improved significantly. But the entire category is benefiting as well: it is taking on more of a premium flavor. Now the challenge is increasingly about brand equity; profits for all competitors that can strengthen equity should rise.

Oscar Mayer is beginning to behave like a high-road brand, and because its category is shifting, that strategy should work well. The company is devoting more money to reinforcing its brand image. For the past two years, for instance, it has sponsored the Super Bowl halftime show—traditionally the bailiwick of high-road products. And it is putting more effort into innovation. Consider the Lunchables product line—a premium convenience product designed for a specific meal. After a slow start, Lunchables has taken off and has been copied by competitors.

In most cases, premium brands competing in value categories do so against a host of regional value brands. Such was the case for Anheuser-Busch, which pursued a low-road strategy during the 1970s and 1980s. In the early 1970s, the beer market sported a number of small, regional value brands. Then, over a 15-year period, Anheuser-Busch reduced its costs and plowed the savings into advertising and lower prices, and consumers began to "trade up" to Budweiser. The once-regional

If a low-road strategy succeeds, the category as a whole may slowly begin to change, as has happened with beer.

beer market began to consolidate, eventually becoming a national business.

If a low-road strategy is successful, the category as a whole may slowly begin to change, as has happened with beer. New, high-end players have entered the market. Several market leaders—including Anheuser-Busch—are now concentrating on innovation. New consumers are being drawn to the category as they become aware of product variations. And increasingly, value-conscious consumers are willing to buy premium brands because they find the higher prices acceptable. Today the entire beer category is becoming more premium: a larger number of companies are competing on brand equity rather than on price.

It may be useful to reiterate the major differences between the high-road and low-road quadrants because, too often, managers of brands with high market share do not differentiate among brands in what are two fundamentally different situations. They pursue the same strategy in both cases and then wonder why their actions are not always rewarding. For low-road brands, cost reduction is critical, SKUs should be reduced, and R&D investments should be aimed at making the manufacturing process more efficient and reducing waste. In the high-road quadrant, cost reduction is not nearly as important, SKU proliferation is desirable, and R&D should focus on product innovation and manufacturing flexibility.

The Dead End: Value Category, Low RMS

Finding a winning strategy in the value-category, low-RMS quadrant is tough, even for those brands that command more than a minimal share of the market. That's why we call them *dead-end brands*. Premium products in this position simply don't make money: they generally earn an ROS of less than 5%. And, unfortunately, many managers of such brands are perennial optimists. "The brand isn't making money today, but it will in the future" is a common, but often misguided, refrain.

The fact is, dead-end brands will never make money. So the choices for managers are limited: either get out of the business or commit to a massive turnaround project, which will move the brand into another quadrant.

One way to "get out of the box" is to slash prices with an eye toward taking share from the market leader (the low-road brand). Such drastic price reduction is usually possible only if the brand is part of a portfolio of products that share internal costs. For example, a dead-end brand can gain ground if managers consolidate package suppliers across an entire portfolio. Another option is outsourcing in areas where the brand isn't large enough to command economies of scale. Or managers might consider bringing together a number of smaller brands in order to gain scale—a move that is commonly called a "string of pearls" strategy.

Heinz Nine Lives canned cat food is one of the best examples we know of a dead-end brand that turned its business around in that manner. Heinz is well known in general for its disciplined approach to cost reduction, but the managers of Nine Lives elevated cost cutting to an art form. After reducing prices several times in the 1980s to compete for share, and after unsuccessfully trying to break the price-war cycle by raising prices in 1991, the managers turned their attention inward. Deciding on a price per can that they believed would be acceptable to consumers, they set out to cut internal costs to meet that goal. They closed eight plants, integrated some of the business vertically (they now make their own cans), and began forming alliances with suppliers.

Heinz Nine Lives already had strong brand equity and access to some inexpensive materials (tuna from the company's Star-Kist business). But it was the dramatic cost reduction that really turned the product around. The brand has been transformed from an also-ran to probably the most profitable product in the category. And Heinz didn't stop there. Once the Nine Lives cost-cutting process was complete, the company went on a pet-food-acquisition binge that more than doubled the size of its business.

Another way to leave the dead-end quadrant—albeit an even more difficult one—is to "trump" the category by introducing a superpremium product that completely resets consumers' expectations. Most often, it takes a new entrant to shake up a category to that extent. Witness how Häagen-Dazs introduced superpremium ice cream into what had been a low-cost, regional market. It is very hard even for established players to follow suit because of the ingrained images of their brands.

The coffee category is also worth another look in this context. Many established manufacturers have recently launched highly differentiated products such as coffee singles and premium roasts. They also are trying to brand coffee sources, such as Java and Colombian, for the first time. Interestingly, such retailers as Starbucks, the Coffee Connection, and Peet's provided the catalyst for change: in effect, they played the role of new entrant to the market, and the credit for resetting expectations lies with them. It remains to be seen whether the established manufacturers can successfully follow their lead.

The biggest mistake that managers make in the dead-end quadrant is hanging on to a brand for years without seriously asking the following questions: Can I become the low-road player through scale and cost reduction? Do I have a prayer of "trumping" this category? If the answers are no, the managers should sell or shut down the brand.

Managing a Portfolio of Premium Brands

In addition to setting strategic imperatives for individual brands, our matrix can help managers better understand the dynamics of a portfolio of products. By plotting their portfolio on the matrix, managers can see which brands are performing up to potential and adjust their expectations for individual brands—and their overall resource allocation—accordingly.

For example, R&D funds should be heavily skewed toward high-road and hitchhiker businesses and should focus on innovation. Often, managers who are overseeing a portfolio spend a disproportionate amount of R&D money on dead-end brands, believing that they can spark a turnaround. Usually, such spending is futile; the money is better spent in areas that promise a decent investment return.

R&D funds should be heavily skewed toward high-road and hitchhiker businesses and should focus on innovation.

Big-ticket media campaigns that are designed to build equity should be saved for high-road and hitchhiker brands as well. For low-road brands, spending on marketing should be limited largely to trade and consumer promotions—activities that lower a product's price. Of course, if managers are trying to change a category's dynamics and turn a low-road brand into a high-road brand, spending more to build equity can be justified. It's a judgment call, and it's all about timing. The important thing is to be aware of the implications of any action—and to resist the urge to spend money where it won't do any good. When considering a portfolio of brands, managers will be tempted to spend too much on marketing for dead-end brands. But throwing promotional money at the trade—offering discounts to supermarkets in exchange for product promotion, for example—simply won't work. It's far better to limit spending on dead-end products and move funding to brands in other quadrants.

Capital spending for dead-end products should be limited as well. As we've said, for low-road and dead-end brands, the focus should be on cost reduction. It would be better to use capital resources to bolster innovation for high-road and hitchhiker brands. Spending money on reducing a product's time-to-market and on flexible manufacturing to churn out short-run SKUs is also worthwhile for high-road and hitchhiker brands. Again, managers must be aware of the possible consequences of any investment.

As we've stressed throughout, category dynamics can change. One of the brands in a portfolio may be a classic hitchhiker, and a competitor's move may cause the entire category to shift from premium to value almost overnight. Beer, once a value category, is now premium. The same goes for athletic footwear. Sneakers were once a value buy; now the category is solidly premium.

The matrix is not meant to be a onetime tool. Managers must reexamine individual brands and entire portfolios on a regular basis. Only by doing so can they successfully prepare for or initiate category shifts and, in the process, help their organizations maximize profitability by coalescing around innovation- and cost-driven businesses.

Originally published in May–June 1997
Reprint 97311

About the Contributors

DAVID A. AAKER, the E.T. Grether Professor of Marketing Strategy at the Haas School of Business, University of California, Berkeley, has published over 80 articles and 10 books, including *Building Strong Brands, Managing Brand Equity, and Developing Business Strategies.* A winner of the 1996 Paul D. Converse Award for outstanding contributions to the development of the science of marketing, Professor Aaker is an active speaker and consultant throughout the world on brand architecture and brand strategy issues.

DAVID HARDING is a director in the Boston office of Bain & Company, where he is a leader in the areas of corporate strategy and organizational effectiveness. He has worked with several of the world's leading consumer-goods companies, as well as leading utility, manufacturer, engineering, and construction companies. Prior to joining Bain & Company, Mr. Harding was a Certified Public Accountant with Arthur Andersen & Company. He earned an MBA from Harvard Business School and a Bachelor of Business Administration from the University of Cincinnati.

ERICH JOACHIMSTHALER is the chairman of Prophet Brand Strategy, a strategic management consulting firm with offices in San Francisco and New York. He is also a visiting professor of business administration at the Darden Graduate School of

Business Administration, University of Virginia, and a William Davidson Research Fellow of the University of Michigan.

DAVID KENNY is the CEO of Bronner Slosberg Humphrey, a relationship marketing company whose mission is to provide a wide variety of world-class capabilities in support of the seminal changes that have shifted the focus of marketing from selling products to servicing customers. Prior to joining Bronner Slosberg Humphrey in 1996, he was a senior partner at Bain & Company. Mr. Kenny holds a BS from General Motors Institute and an MBA from Harvard Business School.

JONATHAN MARK is a director in the Boston office of Bain & Company, where he is one of the leaders of Bain's Private Equity Group. Previously, he led the firm's consumer products practice and was instrumental in developing its groundbreaking work in loyalty-based marketing and Bain's portfolio approach to brand management. Mr. Mark earned an MBA from Harvard Business School and a Master of Science from Technion in Haifa, Israel. He is a graduate of the University of Cape Town in South Africa, where he received a Bachelor of Science in Computer Science and Mathematical Statistics.

REGINA FAZIO MARUCA is a senior editor at the *Harvard Business Review*.

JOHN A. QUELCH is Dean of London Business School and a professor at London University. He was formerly the S.S. Kresge Professor of Marketing at Harvard Business School. An expert on consumer goods and global marketing, he sits on the boards of four public companies in the United States and the United Kingdom.

VIJAY VISHWANATH is a director in the Boston office of Bain & Company, where he leads Bain's Consumer Products Practice. Prior to joining Bain, Mr. Vishwanath worked at Procter

& Gamble. He has written on a variety of consumer-product issues and earned an MBA from Harvard Business School and a Bachelor of Science in Chemical Engineering from the University of Texas at Austin.

Note: *Information provided within each article about the contributors to case studies and perspectives was applicable at the time of original publication.*

Index

Aaker, David A., 72–74,
143–144, 145
Adidas, 18–19
advertising agencies, 5
advertising campaigns. *See*
marketing strategy
Advil, 178
Alexander L. Biel & Associates,
137
alliances, and premium brand
growth, 71, 77
Allman, Carol, 153–156
American Express Optima
card, 108
Anheuser-Busch, 181–182
Apple's Newton computer,
138–139
Aquafresh toothpaste, 114
Arm & Hammer baking-soda
toothpaste, 130
Armani Exchange, 101
automobile industry, 130,
174–175
Avon cosmetics, 123

Balson, John B., 141–143, 146
Bartles & Jaymes, 139

Beatty, David R., 128, 133–135,
145
Benetton, 13–14
Biel, Alexander L., 137–139, 145
biomarketing, 133–134
Black & Decker, 110
DeWalt line, 94
Quantum line, 96, 102
BMW, 94
Body Shop, 1, 20, 21, 22
brand identity at, 6–7
business strategy at, 4
customer involvement in
brand building at, 14–15
Booz-Allen & Hamilton, 156
Borden, 33
Brabeck, Peter, 4
brand awareness, 13, 132, 164
brand building
brand identity and, 5–10
brand visibility and, 10–14
business strategy and, 4–5
customer involvement in,
14–19
development of alternative
approaches to, 19–21
downscaling and, 83–84

193

brand building (*continued*)
  premium brand growth and,
    69–70
  rebuilding strategies and,
    150–153
brand equity. *See also* brand
    loyalty; sub-brands
  brand rebuilding and,
    156–157, 162–163
  brand strategy and, 179, 180
  brand strength and, 30–31,
    138–139
  downscaling risks and,
    82–83, 85–86
  impact of line extensions
    on, 139–141, 145–146
  investment in, 39
  measures of, 2, 21
  premium brand growth and,
    66–68, 75–76
brand growth, and premium
    brands, 51–78
brand identity system, 66–67
brand image. *See* core brand
    identity
brand loyalty, 106, 108,
    111–112, 122–123
  brand management and,
    132–133
  brand rebuilding and,
    162–163, 164
brand-management career
    path, politics of, 132,
    145–146
brand personality, 74, 90
brand strategy
  advertising agencies and, 5

brand growth and, 77
brand rebuilding and, 156
business strategy and, 4–5
execution of, 158–159
premium-brand profitability
    and, 74–75
for premium brand with
    high market share,
    175–179
for premium brand with low
    market share, 174–175
for value brand with high
    market share, 179–182
for value brand with low
    market share, 182–185
Brandweek survey, 41–42
bridge brand strategy, 71–72
Buitoni, 1, 4, 16–18, 21
Burke, James, 39
business strategy, and brand
    strategy, 4–5

Cadbury, John, 15
Cadbury-Schweppes, 1, 15–16,
    21
Cadillac, 83
Campbell, William, 59–62
cannibalization
  downscaling risks and,
    83–84, 90, 91
  line extensions and, 108,
    112, 141–142
  measurement of, 131
  premium brand growth
    strategy and, 76
  private-label production
    and, 33, 38

Casa Buitoni Club, 17–18
Casale, Frank, 57–58, 65
category
  brand profitability and,
    170–172, 175–176
  demand within, and line
    extensions, 112, 113, 115,
    129
  private-label threat and, 29,
    45–47, 48–49
  profit pool and, 46–47
  shifting of, 180–181, 185
  "trumping" the, 184
cereal category, 174
Cheerios, 143
Chrysler, 106, 121, 130, 175
Circuit City, 82
CitiBank, 98–99
Classic Cola, 25, 48
Clorox, 176
Coca-Cola Company, 48, 136,
    141, 178–179
co-driver strategy, 87, 90–91, 96
coffee industry, 96–97, 137,
    170–171, 173–174, 184
Cole, Kim (fictional manager),
    56–58, 76
Colgate toothpaste, 110, 130
"common benefit exploitation,"
    142
company capabilities, and
    competitive advantage,
    20–21
competitors
  brand rebuilding strategy
    and, 158–159
  entry barriers and, 144, 178

complexity, costs of, 116
CompuServe U.K. Shopping
    Centre, 19
Conner, Scott (fictional man-
    ager), 56–58, 64, 69–70
consumer behavior research.
    See market research
Consumer Corporation (fic-
    tional company), 34,
    37–38, 41, 47
consumer database, 17–18. *See
    also* customers
core brand identity
  brand identity system and,
    66–67
  brand rebuilding and,
    164–165
  clarification of, 2, 5–10
  components of brand image
    and, 137
  line extensions and,
    135–136, 137–141
  visibility of, 2, 10–14,
    21–22n, 67–68
core products, 118
cost accounting, 106, 116,
    121–122, 131. *See also*
    internal control systems
cost-cutting measures, 180,
    183–185. *See also* pricing
costs
  of brand launch *vs.* line
    extension, 109
  hidden, 106, 114–117, 129,
    145
  of line extensions, 106, 109,
    114–117, 129

costs (*continued*)
    private-label production
        and, 33–36
Cott Corporation, 25, 48
Courtyard by Marriott hotels,
    73, 87, 89, 100, 108
Craftsman, 31–32
Crest toothpaste, 110, 130
Crowne Plaza hotels, 93
customer equity. *See* brand
    equity
customers. *See also* brand loy-
    alty; consumer database;
    retailers
    brand rebuilding strategy
        and, 158, 162–164
    brand strength and, 30,
        138–139
    expansion of customer base
        and, 143
    involvement in brand build-
        ing, 14–19
    line extensions and,
        107–108, 141–142
    needs of, 70, 107–108,
        141–142, 155
    premium brand pricing poli-
        cies and, 59–60, 62–64
    resistance from, 85, 93–94

DDB Needham survey, 30
dead-end brands, 182–185
Deighton, John, 162–164
delivery systems, proprietary,
    178
descriptor brand. *See* driver-
    descriptor strategy

DeWalt tools, 94
Diet Coke, 136, 141
direct marketing, 82
direct store delivery (DSD) pro-
    gram, 178
distribution channels. *See also*
    retailers
    brand identity and, 10
    brand rebuilding strategy
        and, 158–159
    downscaling and, 82, 84
    premium brand growth and,
        68–69
    pressure for line extensions
        and, 110
    private-label threat and,
        28–29
    proprietary delivery systems
        and, 178
    relations with channel
        partners and, 106,
        123–124
Dolan, Robert J., 62–66
Doritos corn chips, 130
downscaling, 73–74, 82–93
    brand repositioning and,
        84–87
    new brand introduction
        and, 83–84
    sub-brands and, 87–93
driver-descriptor strategy, 87,
    91–93, 96, 97
Drucker Graduate Manage-
    ment Center, Claremont,
    CA, 68
DSD program. *See* direct store
    delivery program

Eagle Snacks, 179
Eckerd Drug Company, 153
economic conditions
    brand strength and, 30–31
    private-label threat and, 23,
        25
ego, and brand management,
    132
endorser strategy, 87, 88–90
entry barriers, 144, 178
Equitrend survey, 30
Europe. *See also entries for spe-
    cific European brands*
    brand-building strategies in,
        1–21
    private labels in, 8, 27–28
excess capacity, and line exten-
    sions, 108–109

Farggi, 9–10
Farquhar, Peter H., 68–72
Farris, Paul W., 135–137, 145
fighting brands, 40–41
Filene's Basement, 92–93
filler products, 119
flanker strategy, 60–61
Folgers coffee, 170–171,
    173–174
Ford Taurus, 87
Frito-Lay, 178–179

Gallo, 138
    Ernest and Julio Gallo Vari-
        etals, 102–103
Gap Warehouse, 83
General Electric Company, 36,
    99

General Mills, 144, 174
Gillette Company, 159
    brand strategy at, 176–177
    Good News razors, 73, 87,
        90–91
Glade Air Fresheners, 143–144
Good & Plenty licorice candy,
    164–165
Grand Met. *See* Häagen-Dazs
gray sales, 99

Häagen-Dazs, 1, 4, 20, 21
    brand building at, 14–15
    brand identity and, 1, 4, 7–9
    category "trumping" and,
        184–185
Hanlon, James A., 164–165
Hanson, Beth (fictional man-
        ager), 150–167
Hardie, Bruce G. S., 128,
    129–131, 145
health club category. *See* Tran-
        sition fitness clubs
Heinz, 32, 40
    Nine Lives cat food, 183–184
Hersh, Anita K., 66–68
Hidden Valley salad dressing,
    143
high-road brand, 175–179
Hill, Sam I., 156–159
hitchhiker brand, 174–175
Hobart Company, 89–90, 100
Holiday Inn, 93
Holy, Jochen, 4
Home Depot, 82, 88
Honda, 94
Hugo Boss, 2, 20

Hugo Boss (*continued*)
  brand building at, 14–15
  brand visibility and, 10–11
  business strategy and, 4

IBM Ambra, 83–84
impulse buying, 108
incentive plans, and brand
  management, 132–133
innovation. *See also* product-
  line extensions
  biomarketing and, 133–134
  high-road brand strategy
  and, 176–177, 178
  hitchhiker brands and, 174
  management of, 143–144,
  146
  premium brand growth and,
  69–70, 72, 185
  private-label threat and,
  39–40, 177
Intel Pentium chip, 22
internal control systems, 37.
  See also cost accounting
Internet, and brand building, 19

John Deere Sabre line, 88–89,
  100
Johnson & Johnson, 39
Johnston, Gordon (fictional
  manager), 51–78

Kellogg, 174
Kenmore, 31–32
Kilmer, James V., 131–133
Kimberly-Clark, 177
Kmart, 83

Kodak Funtime film, 73, 91,
  100
Kraft Macaroni & Cheese, 176
Kroger Company, 28

labor relations, 15
Lacrem ice cream, 9–10
Landmark Communications,
  135
La Shampoo (fictional brand),
  147–168
Lawrence, Sandra, 159–162
Leaf Inc. North America, 164
Levi Strauss, 98–99
Lexus, 94
line extensions. *See* product-
  line extensions
Lister Butler (consulting firm),
  66
Loblaws, 27
Lodish, Leonard M., 128,
  129–131, 145
Loews theaters, 98
low-road brand, 179–182
Lysol, 142

Maggi (brand), 18
Marketing Corporation of
  America, 139
marketing strategy. *See also*
  brand building; mass-
  media advertising; sales
  promotions; sponsor-
  ships
  brand rebuilding and, 151,
  155, 156–157, 160,
  161–162, 165, 166–167

evolutionary perspective on,
    133–134
high-road brands and, 179
marketing mix coordination
    and, 106, 123, 160,
    161–162
product portfolio manage-
    ment and, 185–186
market research
growth strategies and, 71
product-line strategy and,
    106, 122–123, 130–131
market share. *See also* relative
    market share
line extensions and, 110
private-labels and, 38, 48–50
profitability and, 169,
    170–171
market trends, and line exten-
    sions, 144–145
Marlboro price cut, 25–26, 59,
    84–86, 175
Marriott International. *See*
    Courtyard by Marriott
    hotels
Mary Kay Cosmetics, 123
mass-media advertising. *See*
    also marketing strategy
agency reliance on, 5
European companies and,
    3–4
as obsolete for brand build-
    ing, 2–3
mass merchandizers, 28–29
Masterlock Lockers and Bikes
    line, 91–92
Maxwell House coffee, 170–171

McDonald's pizza, 141
Medalist from Hobart Com-
    pany, 89, 90, 100
media. *See* mass-media adver-
    tising; press coverage
Mercedes-Benz, 67, 137–138
    C-Class line, 92, 100
Miller Lite, 141
MJB EuroRoast coffee, 96
Mondavi wines, 142
money, and brand manage-
    ment, 132–133
Motley, Carol, 82–83

Nabisco, 134–135, 178–179
national store brands, 47
Nestlé. *See* Buitoni
Neutrogena, 174
niche products, 118–119,
    162–163, 174
Nine Lives cat food, 183–184

Oil of Olay, 172
Old Navy Clothing Company,
    83
organizational brand, 89–90
organizational culture
brand identity and, 6–7
brand rebuilding and,
    150–153, 160–161
premium brand growth
    strategy and, 76–77
Oscar Mayer, 180–181
outsourcing, 183
oversegmentation, 106, 111,
    129
Oxydol laundry detergent, 41

packaging, 148–149, 161
parent-child metaphor, 101,
    133, 137–138
Pepsi Clear, 141
PepsiCo Foods International,
    36
Philip Morris U.S.A. *See also*
    Campbell, William
    fighting brands and, 40
    Marlboro price cut and,
    25–26
pilot testing, 2, 21, 60
Point-of-Purchase Advertising
    Institute, 108
Polaroid USA, 159
Porsche, 67
Portal, Caroline (fictional man-
    ager), 147–165
Post cereals, 174
power, and brand manage-
    ment, 132–133
premium brands
    brand growth and, 51–78
    brand strategy and, 174–179
    low-end, 96–97, 101
    private-label lines as, 27,
    47
    product portfolio manage-
    ment and, 185–187
    profitability and, 169–170
President's Choice, 27, 31, 134
press coverage, 16
price brands. *See* value brands
Price Club, 82
pricing
    brand identity and, 8, 56,
    62–64, 100–101

brand rebuilding and,
    150–151, 154–155, 161,
    167–168
brand repositioning and,
    84–87
breadth of, and line exten-
    sions, 108
category-based strategies
    and, 173, 174, 175,
    177–178, 183
growth of premium brands
    and, 56, 59–60, 62–64
price elasticity curve and,
    43–44, 45
price premiums and,
    100–101
private-label threat and,
    49–50
private-label production
    control of, 37–38
    risks in reliance on, 24, 25,
    31–37
private-label threat
    actions against, 38–48
    brand manufacturers' influ-
    ence on, 23–24, 25, 32–37
    brand strength and, 29–32
    drivers of, 48–50
    growth of market and, 24
    impact of excessive empha-
    sis and, 31–32
    premium products and, 177
    reality of, 23, 24–25, 26–29
Procter & Gamble Company,
    39, 85, 86–87, 106
    strategy at, 120–121,
    170–171, 173–174

product brand, 89–90
product introduction. *See also*
    product-line extensions
    alternative approaches to,
        8–9
    brand identity and, 12–13
    new brands *vs.* line exten-
        sions and, 112
    private-label threat and,
        49
product-line deletions, 106,
    124–125, 138–139,
    145–146, 180
product-line extensions. *See
    also* stock-keeping unit
    proliferation; vertical
    extensions
    brand mission and, 139–140
    brand rebuilding and,
        134–135, 152–153,
        155–156, 157, 163–164,
        165
    as entry barrier, 144, 178
    expert views on logic
        behind, 127–146
    failures in, 138–139,
        141–142
    growth of premium brands
        and, 56–59, 60–62, 65–66,
        67, 70–78
    hidden costs and, 106,
        114–117, 129, 145
    private-label threat and,
        39–40
    reasons for, 105, 107–110,
        143–144
    risks in, 79–81, 110–117

snack-foods company case
    and, 117–120
    strategic agendas for,
        120–125, 142–143
profitability
    line extensions and, 114,
        124–125, 130
    market share and, 169–171
    measurement of, and cate-
        gories, 46–47
    premium brands and,
        169–172
    private-label production
        and, 37–38
    strategic matrix and, 173,
        174–185
profits-with-a-principle philos-
    ophy, 6–7

quality, and private-label
    threat, 26–27

"Rambo" marketing, 156
R&D. *See* innovation
"real variety need fulfillment,"
    142
Reddy, Srinivas, 82–83
relative market share (RMS),
    171–174
Remlik Foods, 131
repositioning
    brand rebuilding and,
        155–156
    downscaling and, 84–87
    upscaling and, 95
research and development
    (R&D). *See* innovation

resource allocation
  dead-end brands and, 185,
    186
  line extensions and, 106,
    116, 122, 131
retailers. *See also* distribution
    channels
  brand rebuilding and, 154,
    159
  brand strength and, 31
  power struggle between
    manufacturers and,
    132–133
  private-label threat and,
    41–42, 134
  profitability of line exten-
    sions and, 114
  trade relationships with,
    41–42
return on sales (ROS). *See* prof-
    itability
Rice-A-Roni Savory Classics,
    97
RiceTec, 75
risk
  downscaling and, 82–83,
    85–86, 90, 91
  minimization of, and sub-
    brands, 99–103
  and premium brand growth,
    59–62
  product-line extensions
    and, 79–81, 110–117
  reliance on private-label
    production and, 24, 25,
    31–37
RMS. *See* relative market share

Roddick, Anita, 4, 20
Roper Starch Worldwide sur-
    vey, 30–31
ROS (return on sales). *See* prof-
    itability

Saks Fifth Avenue, 83
sales, and line extensions, 109
sales promotions, 44, 86
sales representatives, and
    brand rebuilding,
    153–154
Sam's American Choice, 47,
    134
Sandhill Group, 141
Sanka coffee, 137
Schlitz beer, 86
Sears, Roebuck & Company,
    31–32, 88–89, 95
seasonal products, 119
segmentation
  oversegmentation and, 106,
    111
  rationale for line extensions
    and, 107
senior managers, and brand-
    building strategy, 2, 4–5,
    20, 157–158, 162
shelf-allocation models,
    135–136
Shelman, Mary, 75–78
Sheraton Hotels, 67
Shin, Marni (fictional man-
    ager), 152–153, 155, 157
SKU proliferation. *See* stock-
    keeping unit prolifera-
    tion

SMH company. *See* Swatch
SmithKline Beecham, 114
Snacko (fictional company),
117–120, 135–136
social responsibility, 15
soft-drink industry, 130. *See
also entries for specific
companies*
Sony, 97–98
sponsorships
brand strategy and, 181
brand visibility and, 10–11,
12–13
product introduction and,
8–9
stock-keeping unit (SKU) proliferation, 110, 131–132,
178. *See also* product-line
extensions
strategic matrix, and profitability, 173, 174–185
portfolios of products and,
185–187
of premium brands with
high market share,
175–179
of premium brands with low
market share, 174–175
of value brands with high
market share, 179–182
of value brands with low
market share, 182–185
"string of pearls" strategy,
183–184
sub-brands
downscaling and, 73–74,
87–93, 99–101

risk minimization with,
99–103
upscaling and, 95–97,
101–103
Swatch, 2, 4, 20, 21
brand-building at, 14–15
brand visibility and, 11–13

Taco Bell, 85
Tesco, 99
theme-park strategy, 15–16
Tide detergent, 39, 87
toothpaste category, 110, 114,
130
Toscani, Olivieri, 14
Toyota, 93–94
trade relationships
line extensions and,
112–114
private-label threat and,
41–42
Transition fitness clubs (fictional company)
brand growth at, 59–78
competitive challenges and
responses at, 51–59
"trumping," 184–185
Tylenol, 178

Uncle Ben's Country Inn rice,
95, 97
United Airlines' United
Express, 91
upscaling, 93–97, 101–103
brand repositioning and, 95
credibility and, 93–94
differentiation and, 102

upscaling (*continued*)
  new brand introduction
    and, 94
  sub-brands and, 95–97
urban culture programs, 18–19

value brands
  profitability and, 169–170
  strategies for, 179–185
vertical extensions. *See also*
  downscaling; product-
  line extensions; upscaling
  attractions of, 79, 80
  downscale markets and,
    82–93, 99–101
  market range and, 97–99
  risks of, 79–81

sub-brand strategies and,
    99–103
  upscale markets and, 93–97,
    101–103
Virgin, 18–19
visibility, and brand building,
    10–14

Wal-Mart Stores, 28, 30, 82
Weight Watchers, 132
Weston Foods Ltd., 133
White Cloud toilet tissue,
    40–41
Wicke, Laura S., 128, 139–141,
    145
Woolf, Eric (fictional man-
    ager), 150–165, 167–168